Oceans
of
Wisdom

Linda J T

BALBOA
PRESS

A DIVISION OF HAY HOUSE

Copyright © 2013 Linda J T.

All rights reserved. No part of this book may be used or reproduced by any means, graphic, electronic, or mechanical, including photocopying, recording, taping or by any information storage retrieval system without the written permission of the publisher except in the case of brief quotations embodied in critical articles and reviews.

Balboa Press books may be ordered through booksellers or by contacting:

Balboa Press
A Division of Hay House
1663 Liberty Drive
Bloomington, IN 47403
www.balboapress.com
1-(877) 407-4847

Because of the dynamic nature of the Internet, any web addresses or links contained in this book may have changed since publication and may no longer be valid. The views expressed in this work are solely those of the author and do not necessarily reflect the views of the publisher, and the publisher hereby disclaims any responsibility for them.

The author of this book does not dispense medical advice or prescribe the use of any technique as a form of treatment for physical, emotional, or medical problems without the advice of a physician, either directly or indirectly. The intent of the author is only to offer information of a general nature to help you in your quest for emotional and spiritual well-being. In the event you use any of the information in this book for yourself, which is your constitutional right, the author and the publisher assume no responsibility for your actions.

Any people depicted in stock imagery provided by Thinkstock are models, and such images are being used for illustrative purposes only. Certain stock imagery © Thinkstock.

ISBN: 978-1-4525-7233-8 (sc)
ISBN: 978-1-4525-7235-2 (hc)
ISBN: 978-1-4525-7234-5 (e)

Library of Congress Control Number: 2013906624

Printed in the United States of America.

Balboa Press rev. date: 04/25/2013

Contents

Acknowledgments xiii

Introduction xv

Part 1: Pleasures of the ocean

Oceans of wisdom 3

Ocean 4

Let the ocean worry 5

The wonder of the ocean 7

The wonder of the earth 8

This beautiful earth 9

The ocean has much play in her and much to teach us 10

My life 11

Oceanic Experience 14

The power of the ocean 16

Treasures from the ocean 18

Sand castles 19

Imagination 20

Sing your song 22

My mother 24

My father 25

There is no end to the wonder of the sea 27

Journey of the waters 28

When we're at the beach, we forget to count the days 29

Declare national "get to the beach" day 30
Nature 31
Take a walk 33
The ocean is a mystery..34
Beach life is good..35
Sunset 36
Beach time 37
The beach cures you..38
Collecting shells..39
It's a wonderful life 40
Quiet time on the beach 42
The art of healing..43
May we be walking beaches together for the
    rest of our lives... 44
Finding inner peace at the beach...............................45

Part 2: Ocean wisdom

Special moments in your life.....................................49
Seashore of the mind...50
Music for the heart 51
God's love notes 52
Wake...53
Rushing to calmer seas 55
Loneliness 57
On land or at sea 58
Keep your life simple..59

Sunrise	60
Every day is a new sunrise	61
Rainbows	62
Watching the ocean	65
One must find one's self before one can lose it	66
Do not disturb	67
Setting the right course	68
Is the glass half empty or half full?	70
Checking in with yourself every day	71
Life is like the ocean flowing	72
How do we raise our sails to inner silence?	73
The purpose of life	74
There's no time like the present	76
Happiness	78
All we need is love	80
The ripples of life	82
If you're lucky enough to be at the beach, you're lucky enough	84
To be true to yourself	86
The joy of growth	87
Journey	89
The journey of a thousand miles begins with a single step	90
Jigsaw puzzle of life	91
People who come into your life for a reason, a season, or a lifetime	93
Sing your song	95

Wind clears our heads of clouds	97
Clear as water	98
Try to keep your head above water	99
Waves	100
Rewards from the sea	101
With all sails set	102
Living words	103
Resentment	104
Water	105
Calming the inner sea	106
Discovering the sand dollar	107
Wisdom in us	108
Doing nothing else, looking at the ocean	109
The power and glory of the ocean	110
A great sailor story	111
A clean ship is a happy ship	112
Are you lost at sea, or have you missed out on the direction you have sailed?	113
Create a quiet place	114
Ideas in your mind	115
Making your dreams come true	117
Open the prison door	119
The sea of inner peace	120
Weathering the storm of life	122
Go with the flow	123
Soul searching	125

Inner silence at the beach 126
Wonder of the shore 127
The calm before the storm 128
It's never too late to change your course in life 129
Follow your inner compass 130
"The Winds of Fate" 131
Strong feelings are like thunderstorms 132
Your life is waiting 133
Let the waves of the ocean carry us 135
Rhythm of life 136
Energy Surfing 137
Cranio-Sacral expresses as a rhythmic
    motion just like the ocean 139
Take the ride of your life with the flow and balance 143
Floating on the ocean in a raft 144
Life on the beach is your playground 146

Part 3: Life at the beach

Vacations 149
Spring break 152
Sunrise 153
Every day is a new sunrise 154
Swimming the ocean 155
Walking and jogging on the beach 156
Watching Sunsets 157
Solitude 158

Time for me 159
Ocean ritual 160
Conch shells 162
Life on the ocean wave 163
Tranquility 164
Beach walk 166
Just relax and listen to the waves 168
An undersea effect to help children sleep 169
A dolphin story 170
A little bird story 171
A duck story 172
A little starfish story 174

Part 4: Ocean facts and creatures

Boat facts 179
Natural navigation 180
A little fish story 181
Sandpipers 183
A big shark story 184
Humpback whales 185
Seahorses 186
Lobster and shrimp 187
Dolphins 188
Eagles 189
Horseshoe crabs 190

Pelicans 191
Ocean birds 192
The moon 193
Minnesota Snowbirds.. 194

Part 5: Life's good: The ocean is calling you!

Sailing 199
Kayaking... 201
Surfing.. 203
Snorkeling 204
Coral reefs.. 206
Enjoy a massage on the beach................................. 207
Craniosacral therapy in the ocean............................ 209
Meditation by the beach 211
Breathing on the beach.. 212
Yoga by the ocean 214
Riptide.. 216
Undertow.. 217
Seasickness... 218
No-see-ums 220

When was the last time you really looked at the ocean?...... 221
About the author..223

Acknowledgments

My gratitude goes out to

Loretta, for her help in editing this book, for her wonderful friendship and support, and for the wonderful weeks and days spent with her in Cocoa Beach, Florida, at her condo by the ocean.

Greg, for his friendship, partnership, and love, and also for the great support he has given me.

All of my clients, for being my friends and for all the help and support they have given me.

All of my wonderful friends and family for their support and understanding.

And the ocean, the most everlasting teacher that nature ever created and the gift that it has given to me. Thank you.

Introduction

Most of us don't have the luxury of living by the ocean or visiting the beach on vacation. But using this book about the ocean, we can access mental images and visualize the ocean. In this book I hope to capture truths about life that make sense to us all, not to challenge the intellect but to touch the soul. Just reading a chapter or a quote every morning or night feeds your soul. I hope that this book speaks to you in a special way. It seeks to capture the essence of the mind and to share the oceans of wisdom with you and the world.

I wish to help save the oceans and to improve life for the betterment of all. The important thing is to do something, even if it's as simple as making the earth a cleaner place or learning to listen to oceans of wisdom. Just stop to think what is happening to the place we call home and what you can do to make it a better place to live. It's up to us to save some of these amazing places so that our children today can go to them in the future. Those who live near the waters know that this land is special, and I know it as well. The ocean helps us to return to the days when life was simpler and safer and when spirits soared. It recalls a time when the future meant tomorrow and the next day was the next day. I believe that time spent reading, being in nature at the beach, getting a massage, or meditating is time for the soul.

What a gift it would be to take a trip back in time and revisit the good old days. I have seashells as remembrances of the oceans I have visited. I keep a collection from each beach I have been to. When I was very young, I started having a calling toward the sea. I didn't really understand it all that much; I just knew that I needed to be near the ocean and its life. All the thoughts are memories for my book. My bucket list is to see every ocean and beach I can see.

Part 1

Pleasures of the ocean

Oceans of wisdom
A prayer for the ocean

"To stand at the edge of the ocean is to have knowledge of things that are as eternal as any earthly life can be."

—Rachel Carson

Look to the oceans for treasures. My treasure chest is filled with shells, memories, and a lot of great wisdom and thoughts that have given me great relief, joy, and happiness.

To remember that life is as the ocean itself, ever changing, is to understand that we cannot control everything. The ocean is the greatest teacher for me and everyone who will listen to it. We are all thirsty for wisdom and information that can help us have a better life.

The ocean calms us down so we can think more clearly. Just breathing the ocean air makes us feel a little lightheaded and a lot happier. The ocean has many moods. The ocean reminds us to be fluid and flow with life. It helps us to remember that everything has a rhythm and to respect natural cycles.

Ocean

**Go to the ocean and listen to the music of
the waves; the ocean is talking to you.**

The ocean has secrets to tell. There is a voice in the water of the great sea, and it calls us continually. Sometimes it calls when the waves are smashing high against the shore, as if to force our attention. Sometimes it whispers in the calm. But whether the ocean comes in crashing or in a gentle stillness, its voices speak to us. The sea has much to say, and just by listening to such notes you can hear the wonder of the sea. When the oceans are full of peace and tranquility, the air is clean and pure, and the sky is clear also. When the ocean is calm, the whole earth is covered with a sudden happy moment.

We all have oceans of pleasures.

Let the ocean worry
"Life is not a problem to be solved
but a mystery to be lived."
—Unknown Author

Have you ever heard the saying, "Let the ocean worry"? I think it has been doing that for many years. The ocean and its treasure has been a great gift from God to humans for many years. But modern man destroys all nature's treasure for his greed. It takes billions of creatures millions of years to build a coral reef, yet mankind can destroy them every day. Anyone who spends time in and on the sea will tell you of all the plastic garbage distributed through the water column. It is a lot of garbage with little chance of being cleaned up. The outer pollution will never stop until we address the inner pollutions. Someday the fish will not be able to swim in our polluted water. Then what will we eat? Think about the quality of the water we drink. Are we going to sit back and ask why in the world this is happening to us?

Think of all the tsunamis, hurricanes, flooding, earthquakes, etc. The earthquakes happened for a reason, science tells us, and the tsunamis likewise. There have been a lot of them lately.

Ask if the ocean has a message for you each day, if things get uncomfortable enough around us to wake us up. In awakening, we start to develop our potential to act like human beings.

Everyone should start caring about what is happening to this beautiful world we call home. Wisdom is knowing the source of things. Sometimes we need to be at the ocean, to really see the ocean from a different perspective.

The wonder of the ocean

"The larger the island of knowledge, the longer the shoreline of wonders."

—Ralph W. Sockman

I can remember listening to the ocean for hours as it initially crashed around me and then gradually smoothed into a murmur. My body relaxed into the earth and into myself. The world seemed far away, and there was no need to bring it closer. Wonder is a gift of living. Living is a gift of wonder. Just being by the ocean heals the soul. The ocean of life is living with its abundance. The wonder of the ocean is everywhere.

The wonder of the earth
I wonder where our wonder is?

The earth holds so many wonders. We can experience great wonder if we only let ourselves feel the earth, live in it, and understand it more. We have taken the earth for granted for a long time. The earth puts us in our place, yet we are destroying the earth with pollution, toxic waste, oil spills, and trash, just to name a few. We need to thank the earth, for it feeds, clothes, houses, and sustains us. We should think of our earth as something that is alive, something that breathes with the great masses of air circulating about it, something that nourishes itself with a terrific circulatory system of water being evaporated from the oceans and deposited on parched soil, and something that rebuilds itself through an endless process of breaking down and rebuilding its structural system through deterioration of rock to sand to soil and back to rock.

This beautiful earth

"Don't ask yourself what the world needs: ask yourself what makes you come alive and then go and do that. Because what the world needs are people who have come alive."
—Howard Thurman

Just lying on the earth (without padding) does something for us. Listening to the earth and hearing the counsel of silence gently speaks to each of us in the infinite language of all life. Where is your wonder and humility toward the earth? Start where you are, and see what you can contribute toward environmentalism within you. Living consciously is one of the greatest gifts we can give to ourselves and to our children. Maybe it is time to take the children and ourselves to the beach for a trash cleanup. It helps the environment and also gives children a lesson on how we all can help save the earth. Conscious giving means thinking outside the wallet.

The ocean has much play in her
and much to teach us

Whether you love surfing, fishing, or eating fish, you need to start paying attention to the ocean. Seventy percent of the world's oxygen comes from the ocean, and how do we say thank you? The ocean is the most powerful force on the planet. It feeds us and those all around us. Why are we not protecting it? All of the fish, whales, dolphins, crabs, and sea birds, just to name a few, make their living in or near the ocean.

My life

"My life is like a stroll upon the beach,
As near the ocean's edge as I can go."
—Henry David Thoreau

For me, the beach has always been truly home since I was very little. I was born in San Diego, California. I always felt that the ocean was calling for me to do something. I did not know what then, but now I think it was to write this book. I feel that it is my purpose to write this book now, for whatever reason. I think this might reach someone's life the way the ocean talks to me.

Growing up in San Diego, I always went to the beach. I still remember how quickly I fell in love with the smell of salty air, the roar of the crashing waves on the shore, and the sand between my toes. As teenagers, all of my friends and I would head down to Atlantic City, New Jersey. This was before there was gambling there. We would rent bikes in the early morning and ride on the boardwalk, and we would sometimes go horseback riding on the beach. At night, we might drive to Margate and listen to the bands. I was fascinated by all the different seashells. It was then I began my hobby of collecting seashells, always looking for something new and different. I was always amazed at how unique each one was.

So many other events in my life have been an unsettling mystery. I have spent years wondering what might have been.

I have spent hundreds of hours staring into the ocean, waiting for the answers to rush over me in the salt air. Sometimes I have searched with nothing to show for my efforts, and sometimes I have missed opportunities for life changes. Isn't that the story of all of our lives, though? We are always looking for that perfect someone, that perfect job, or that perfect situation, but they never quite arrive. Does perfection really exist after all?

When I look back to being a child, where were my happiest moments and memories? At the beach, of course! I use to write my troubles on the sand. I wrote several words in the sand, and then as the tide washed them away, I always wished my troubles away. Most of the time, my troubles would go away with the tide! The ocean is and always will be a big part of my life. Fascination with the ocean will always be a part of me. I was always an early riser, watching the sunrise and collecting the best shells on the beach. Watching the waves rumble onto the shore and collecting my thoughts along the way is the finest way to begin my day.

What's more, the ocean landscape, which extends as far as my eyes can see, always reminds me of endless opportunities in my life. At the ocean I can listen to my inner voice, shed my thoughts, be with the rhythm of the waves, and ask my soul for some unanswerable questions. There is no more doubt that the ocean is in my blood than that there is sand in my toes. It was at the ocean that I spent my childhood days, and it keeps calling me to this day. I always feel at peace when I am at the ocean. It is as if I am possessed by the ocean, the beaches, the boardwalk in Atlantic City, and the feeling of peace and of oneness that has comes over me. The ocean and I are soul mates.

The beach to me is a sacred place between the earth and the ocean, one of those places where life can be experienced, where endings can be lived and beginnings seen. A walk along the beach offers unexpected gifts for me, especially when I see treasure in the form of beautiful seashells that are teased by the tides. As I walk, I can scan the horizon and glimpse the endless opportunities that life has given me. Feeling a sense of adventure, I dive into the water and experience the rush of the waves hitting me.

Being by the ocean gets me out of my head and into my body and soul. One of the most significant gifts of the beach is seeing the world from a different place and reviewing the world of wisdom. Being at the beach teaches me to lean on my senses and feel the intensity of the ocean experience that is trying to tell me something. Learning about life is very beneficial, and the ocean gives me an opportunity to do so. It also gives us an understanding of what is happening in the world around us.

> **"He that will learn to pray, let him go to the sea."**
> **—George Herbert**

Oceanic Experience
"Have you ever experienced a spiritual force that seems to lift you out of yourself?"
Andrew Greeley

Oceanic experience. The experience usually brief and completely unexpected, of being at one with the entire universe, and of feeling a deep meaning and purpose to every part of existence. It is often accompanied by feeling of compassion and love for all beings. (Source from The Concise Oxford Dictionary of World Religions, 1997, John Bowker)

This is my experience of what is called an Oceanic experience. It started when I was very young, at the ocean, which then I could not describe it in words. It was not until I got older, after having a lot of these Oceanic experiences. Most of them when I was at the ocean, at an inspiring sunrise or sunset, or around trees and their roots, a powerful waterfall, and sometimes even listen to the songbirds.

Having an Oceanic experience is like going on an adventures trip to nowhere land. Some people call it lalla lalla land, but the only good thing is that you remember the experience and just being awed by the experience that has existed. It's very hard to describe but it's like that instant feeling that you are part of everything around you, a force that seems to lift you out of yourself. I also think the Oceanic experience is a state of consciousness and a real perception of what is really going on around you and the world. It is a feeling of something limitless, emotional and is something that is beyond words can define. It's a personal connection with your personal being, and the reality of the inner world, and you will have a greater balance within our planet. I also think this can only happen when you feel empty enough to take it all in.

I have had these Oceanic experiences several times in my life, and will never forget the life changing experiences that they have had on me.

I hope that everyone can experience this Oceanic experience in their lifetime. It's a really awe moment one that you will never forget.

The power of the ocean
"You will learn a life's worth of lessons from the ocean."
—Unknown Author

The power of the ocean demands respect. The ocean doesn't realize its own energy, and it sometimes can be overpowering. The ocean knows us better than we know ourselves. The ocean will never disappoint you and disappear; you can count on its existence and its loyalty. As you walk along the shores of the ocean and enjoy a little solitude, it caresses your feet, but even more, it caresses your tired soul. Open your heart to the magic found at the water's edge. The ocean will see to it that you forget what you have left behind. The ocean has no ideals, no standards, and no measurements. It is free, wild, and freeing. It shows us our potential and points us to our true destinies. The longer you look at the ocean, the more you will see. No matter where we are, we'll always be connected by the ocean. The ocean will always remain a place of infinite beauty and mystery.

Remember that life is as the ocean itself, ever changing, and understand that you cannot control everything. The ocean also gives us permission to explore new possibilities and new ways of participating in our very alive planet. We are as wild as the ocean, as unpredictable, and potentially as loving. When life gets too complicated, confusing, and overwhelming, being at the ocean gives you a sense of relaxation and rejuvenation, which also gives you a sense of peace, if not hope. The ocean isn't to be conquered or controlled; it's to be met where it is. The ocean communicates with feeling and in silence. The ocean is magic; we are all under its spell.

Treasures from the ocean
"Ocean treasures left on the shore,
nature's gifts to adore."
—Unknown Author

Everyone should look to the ocean for treasures. The ocean is filled with treasures. My treasure chest is brimming with shells, memories, and a lot of great wisdom and thoughts that have given me great relief, joy, and happiness. Have you found the treasure map that holds all the answers for you? It is never too late to start looking for it. Beaches are places of mystery and wonder, waiting to be explored. Spending time by the ocean is a treasured experience, something we never forget.

Sand castles

**"Reminders of the carefree days,
building castles in the sand."**

—D. Morgan

I know a lot about sand castles, and so do a lot of children. Watch them and you will learn. Go build a sand castle, but build one with a child's heart. When the sun sets and the tides wash the sand castle away, salute to a lovely day. I remember when I was very young, I was at the beach building a big sand castle. A younger girl came up to me and told me I was using up all the sand on the beach. I thought that was so funny.

"Even castles made of sand fall into the sea eventually."

—Jimi Hendrix

Imagination

"There are no rules of architecture for castles in the clouds."
—Gilbert K. Chesterton

As a child, I would lie on the beach looking at the clouds and see never-ending images of sailing ships, clown faces, sandcastles, and whatever my thoughts or imagination allowed me to see. What a wonderful thing our imagination is. A child can look at a boat on the sea and imagine great pirate ships sailing over a mighty and endless sea, battling for treasure. A child can be an astronaut, a sailor, a doctor, a solder, or whatever he or she desires! The ability to simply look and see something else is something powerful and awesome, like the ocean and the clouds that form over it.

When we are adults, often the only time our imaginations come into play is when we make up stories about someone or something. Perhaps our imaginations are just so out of practice that they have taken a negative turn. We can hopefully change that. Imagination just asks us to look at a range of ideas or options. Get reacquainted with your creative, imaginative side. We need our imaginations to dream, to be what we can, and to think about what we might become. Our imaginations allow us to free our minds and souls to go to places that we have never been. Let your imagination lift you up out of the muddy path so you can see what is possible in the ocean, the clouds, the stars, life, and wherever our dreams take us.

"Imagination is more important than knowledge."
—Albert Einstein

Sing your song

"A bird does not sing because it has an answer. It sings because it has a song."
—Maya Angelou

Choosing and finding our song is very important. The journey along the way can make the song so much better when it is finally sung. If we do not take notice along our way, we will not gather the right harmony for the full song in our heart. Singing stirs up the soul like nothing else. If your song shows you as being nurturing and forging new directions, then your song will be filled with richness, harmony, and wonderful joy. If you have a song to sing, sing it. What sound bites are pumping into your head? What tune is playing on your iPod? When you go to the ocean, do you hear the theme from Jimmy Buffet's "Margaritaville"? The tune you listen to will conjure up feelings, but which songs make you happy and smile? The tunes you play and the words you say to yourself determine how you see life. Here are some songs that I love to get me in the mood for the beach.

"Toes"—Zac Brown Band
"Don't Worry Be Happy"—Bobby McFerrin
"KoKomo"—The Beach Boys
"Beer in Mexico"—Kenny Chesney
"Margaritaville, "Cheeseburger in Paradise"—Jimmy Buffett

"Don't Drink the Water"—Brad Paisley and Blake Sheldon

"Water"—Brad Paisley

"Sittin' on the Dock of the Bay"—Otis Redding

My mother
"The beach is in our blood. Everyone in our family returns to the beach instinctively, just like the sea."
—Sandy Archibald

My earliest memories are of my mother and me at the beach, from San Diego to Atlantic City. She used to love to sing "Under the Boardwalk" and "September Song." She would stand at the water's edge and explain that a beach very much like the one we were standing on was just over the horizon bordering the same ocean. Her point was that although we couldn't see the other side, the ocean still connected us to the people who lived there. When I was at the beach with my mother, she would say, "No matter where we are, we'll always be connected by the ocean." No matter where we lived, she always longed for that view of the ocean. Mom always said that the salt air makes us hungry. She was right, too; I was always hungry after being in the ocean. She died of breast cancer at the very young age of fifty-eight. She never lived long enough to fulfill her dreams. After my mother died, I found seashells that she had picked up at the beach in her jewelry box. Every time I pick one up, I am so grateful for its reminders of how much she loves the ocean and the gift she has left for me. I have the shells all over the place, along with a picture of her at Atlantic City. She looks like a model.

My father

"Along the beach I never collected shells from my father's shore."
—Corey Hart

My father spend half his life in the US Navy and the other half of his life as a bar owner. At the end of his life, he suffered for years hooked up to an oxygen tank, barely moving in his recliner. He was on constant oxygen and medication. Every breath was a labored struggle. He was barely able to speak and was only able to ingest liquids for food. He had been suffering from cancer for years. Just a week before my father died, I asked him whether the quality of his life was worth all the effort. He said no.

As I walk down the beach, I can't help but wonder what it would be like to have my last wishes stolen from me. My father's last will and testament was not fulfilled. My father said that he did not want an open casket; he wanted people to remember him the way he looked when he was alive. Also, he did not want his ashes to go to Florida with the bugs. He wanted to have his ashes buried at sea in San Diego. That was the last thing he said before he died.

I remember those days when I was very young, when the whole family was traveling and moved every year. When Dad was driving from state to state, I would always ask, "Dad, is there an ocean where we will be living?"

He would always say, "Don't ask again! You will have to wait until we get there." Dad loved keeping us in suspense. We learned never to ask him, "Are we there yet?" Dad really hated that too. The reason he didn't tell us about the ocean is because he loved to see the happy look on our faces when we did see the ocean.

There is no end to the wonder of the sea
"The ocean is a mighty harmonist"
—William Wordsworth

The lure of the sea has enticed explorers to probe the mysteries of that vast, sparkling wilderness. The sea never changes, and its work is for all to see. The ocean is wrapped in mystery. Looking out over the mysterious ocean from the marginal world of the shore, you sense the interchangeability of land and sea. There is also awareness of the past and of the continuing flow of time.

Journey of the waters
"Don't you realize that the sea is the home of water? All water is off on a journey unless it's in the sea, and it's homesick, and bound to make its way home someday."
—Zora Neale Hurston

We are all like water. We are off on a journey to return to ourselves. Some of our journeys have taken us as far as we can go, and many of our days have been absorbed by the sandy riverbanks that contain us. Yet we continue to flow, heavy and swollen in the spring of our lives and often reduced to a trickle as we approach the fall of our years. "Return," we murmur as we tumble over the stones in our path, ever cognizant that although we may wander through new and strange lands, our destination is a return. The ocean water always does return to the sea, just as I have to return to myself.

When we're at the beach, we forget to count the days
"The Sea, once it casts its spell, holds
one in its net of wonder forever."
—Jacques Cousteau

I love to stroll along the beach, watching the view and getting some fresh ocean air. My first sight of the ocean always takes my breath away. It looks cool and inviting, with a blue sky that stretches for miles above the churning edge of sand. The tide laps my toes. I pick up shells as they come onto the shore. I wonder why their goal was to leave the ocean at all. If it were up to me, I think, I never would leave the ocean. The love of the ocean is the love of our life, a love that never leaves us as long as we live. We are like the shells, riding the tides, only to be beached until someone throws us back to sea.

"One cannot collect all the beautiful shells on the beach."
—Anne Spencer

Declare national "get to the beach" day
Laughter is an instant vacation at the beach

I was so surprised when I went to Florida to learn that people who live near a beach never go to the beach. Living in Minnesota, the only whitecaps I see are white caps of the snow drifting beneath my windows or icicles hanging from the roof. I guess that people who do not live near the beach always long to be there, and people who live near the beach never miss being there.

Just think how productive you could be if your company send you to the beach for a day! Your thoughts would help the company. The employees would have less stress and be more productive. Ask your boss to declare "get to the beach" day at your office. Wow, there is a great concept! Take your boss to the beach for lunch.

Nature

"The three great elemental sounds in nature are the sound of rain, the sound of wind in primeval woods, and the sound of outer ocean on a beach."
—Donna McLavy

When you spend time at the beach, floating on a river, paddling on a lake, or surfing the ocean—well, you just *feel* better. Thus you love your time on the earth. Thus you'll do something to show your love. Right?

The more one sees the ocean, the more one can see how far most of us are from living close to nature, from living close to the earth, the oceans, and the sand. There's something about unruly, unpredictable, fickle nature that can attune us to being right here now. Nature offers a miracle cure that soothes the ragged, weary soul and gives us a sense of confidence that all will work out.

How far we live from swimming easily in the waters of the earth! Come closer; come and spend time on the earth. See everything just as it is. Spend quiet time simply being upon the earth as it is—that is, while it is and in exactly the current situation. Contemplating the earth as it is worth your time. It tells you who you are, whence you came, and whither you go. It calls your name and even gives you your name, if you are still near enough to hear it along the paths that lead through and out again to the dunes of the ocean's coast. There is nothing to add now that you awake. You are complete. There's something about the earth and the oceans that brings a sense of awe and even makes a rushing mind ease into a more natural rhythm. The silent harmony of nature waits, ever present. Take a piece of nature with you to carry you through every day.

Take a walk

Experts blame the decline of appreciating nature on video games and the Internet. Our lack of knowledge and commitment to the earth comes at exactly the wrong time, with global warming, polluted air and oceans, poisoned food, and so on. One way to deal with the dismal scenario of an uncommitted citizenry confronting a degenerating Earth is to spend time at the beach, in the mountains, hiking a trail, visiting a park, floating on a river, paddling on a lake, or surfing the ocean until you just feel better. Responsible stewardship of the places we visit is essential. Stewardship implies responsibility and the realization that we are visitors here. Our commitment and pledge should be to let anyone passing this way do no harm. Live in accord with nature, and if you are satisfied there will be no wanting in your life. This will bring you great joy. We can always hope.

> **"The earth seems to rest in silent meditation; and the waters and the mountains and the sky and the heavens seem all to be in meditation."**
> **—Chandogya Upanishad**

The ocean is a mystery
"Mystery creates wonder, and wonder is the basis of man's desire to understand."
—Neil Armstrong

I love being out in nature and coming upon an ocean that grabs me and my heart. My appreciation of the ocean dates back to my childhood with my mother, a sailor's wife left home to wander when my father was out to sea. Even as a child I could tell if the ocean was sad or happy. The nature of the ocean beckons me. It is just because of its mystery. The ocean knows what happiness is without a struggle. If you can see the magic of the ocean, then you will feel an enhanced sense of mystery and love for the ocean. We don't know what the light of the sunrise is without the darkness of the night.

Beach life is good
"Life's good at the beach"
—Unknown author

Every day is special at the beach, from the sunrise to the sunset to the full moon. At the beach you can relax and soak up the sun, watch the waves, and go looking for special seashells. With the sunshine on your face, you can enjoy the sounds of the waves hitting the shore and the calm, cool breeze blowing into your ears. Every hour spent by the beach has a memory of its own that fills your heart with positivity and makes your body feel at ease. There is a lot that we can learn from the beach. To express it all in just four words, *beach life is good.*

Sunset

"Every sunset brings the promise of a new dawn."
—Ralph Waldo Emerson

Notice the spectacular sunset diffusing golden and fuchsia light, turning the ocean into a pool of amber glass! It looks as if an artist dipped his brush in his palette and streaked it across the horizon. How beautiful it is to look at that! Looking at the sunset makes us instantly relaxed, seeing through the eyes of timeless wonder and gratitude. Watching the sun slip below the horizon and watching the sun's descent makes us marvel at the world we live in. As we ponder the sun's parting glory, we realize we are finding joy when not seeking it. This can become a pattern in life. Once you stop longing for the extraordinary things in life and start finding pleasure in everyday things, something spectacular happens to you. Sunset is a place of comfort and encouragement for us as well as a place of beauty. The sunset can cast a bounty on the most impoverished soul. We have all the riches one could hope for right here with the sunset and the sea. We look forward to watching the amazing sunset that fills the sky with vivid splashes of color and feeling the gentle breeze that caresses our face as the sun begins its dip into the sea. The treasured sunset is a bag that bursts with the gold of the dawn.

Beach time
"We all leave footprints in the sand. The question is, will we be a big heal or a great soul?"
—Unknown Author

There is no such thing as time. There is only life, leaving its footprints on the beach. The beach makes it possible to quiet down, rest, and be present, no matter what your circumstances may be. Time at the beach is not a story; it's an experience. You cannot be a beach lover without getting sand between your toes. Time at the beach affects people's lives. At the beach, the sun smiles down, and a thousand waves keep a slow, calming drumbeat in the background. This is the cycle of beach life. The moment we step on the sand, we are transformed for the day. Have you left your footprints on the beach?

"Footprints in the sands of time ... where have you been? Where are you going?
—Jonathan Lockwood Huie
"Don't tell me the sky is the limit; there are footprints on the moon!"
—Unknown Author

The beach cures you
"We must be willing to let go of the life we planned,
so as to accept the life that is waiting for us."
—Joseph Campbell

When you need to return to reality and harmony, the beauty of earth and the sea can be found at the beach. Began your day barefoot and free, running the beaches as far as you can see. Go to the beach and swim the ocean. It will cure you. The beach is a place of healing. When we are by the ocean, the sand, and the sky, even two people can feel as close to each other as their own footprints on the beach. Everything seems timeless and everyone ageless.

In times of crisis, go to the beach. We ponder its majesty and power, reminded that we are only like small grains of sand, as we watch the waves spilling onto shore and continuing on and on. The wonder of God's power calms and soothes us, enabling us to deal with whatever crises life deals us. The ocean shows us a way of being with ourselves and others. Being with the ocean and sky is also a healing experience. We wonder at the stillness of the water and at how the ocean and the sky far above seem to offer support. The ocean and the sky lovingly conform to our healing intention. The power and magic of the beach let us experience relaxation, rejuvenation, inspiration, calmness, and challenge.

Collecting shells
"To find a seashell is to discover a world of imagination."
—Michelle Held

The shells you find are the ones meant for you. To find the best shells, you have to walk slowly. As we walk along the ocean examining the fascinating shells, we are reminded that now is all we have and now is all we need. When we admire seashells, we may have no idea how they are formed. Maybe shells are a symbol for your journey. The scallop shell became a symbol of Saint James for having made the voyage and returned home safely. Shells were found on the seashore not far from the cathedral, and the pilgrims who returned to the interiors of Europe took home these shells as souvenirs to signal to others that they had arrived at the destination. Inspired by this practice, you may want to find a symbol for your journey.

"One cannot collect all the beautiful shells on the beach."
—Anne Morrow Lindbergh

It's a wonderful life

"Some people come into our lives and quickly go. Some stay for a while and leave footprints on our hearts, and we are never, ever the same."

—Author Unknown

Here is a true story. After the death of her mother, a daughter found a bag of shells that her mother had inscribed by hand.

Her mother collected these shells when she was sixty-one and already showing signs of the lung disease that would kill her the next year. They didn't know that then, but they knew that something was wrong and that the mom needed an adventure. Her daughter knew that her mother never took beach vacations and that she loved the seashore, so she took her to the Jersey Shore. When the daughter told her mother that she'd be able to hear the ocean from her window, she started to cry. She had the best time of her life at the shore.

After she died, her daughter found the bag of shells.

Nearly fourteen years later, they're a collective nudge from a mother who never lost her sense of wonder. One by one, the shells are finding a new place in the daughter's home. One is at the computer, and another rests on the windowsill over the kitchen sink. She puts them where she is sure to see them.

Every so often, she picks one up and squeezes it, grateful for the reminder to live a pinch-me attitude about the world.

Source: Connie Schultz, "My Mom's Wonderful, 'Pinch Me' Life," *Parade Magazine*, July 1, 2012.

Quiet time on the beach
"We need quiet time to examine our lives openly and honestly ... spending quiet time alone gives your mind an opportunity to renew itself and create order."
—Susan Taylor

When we walk on the beach, we are enveloped in an aura of peace and serenity. Our spirit and soul become blanketed with the spirit of nature. It is the simple things in life that always bring us back to this realization: "Life is good." After this realization, we have a much deeper appreciation of life's quietness and reassurance. Happiness often sneaks through a door you didn't know you left open.

The ocean promotes freedom of the mind, body, and spirit. The beach provides a kind of relaxation that nudges back the sands of time. It's no surprise that it should be so pleasurable; after all, you started life floating in a warm, private ocean without laundry, bills to pay, or traffic. Your private time at the ocean takes you back there. The time of seaside solitude, enjoying the sound of the waves and the sea breeze, is all that is needed. It only takes minutes of seaside solitude to recharge your flagging batteries and renew your contact with nature. Notice how your minutes of solitude affect the hours of your day. If you have yet to savor this treasure, put it high on your priority list now.

The art of healing

The ocean fires our imaginations and rekindles our spirits. Spend some quiet time by the ocean and you may even find the answers to some of your questions about life. Watch the dolphins and see how much peace they have. That's when I first noticed the change; my whole outlook began to shift. There was something special about those days on the ocean water. I was inspired by the creatures of the sea, even the baby manatee. She had a tranquility that I'd never seen before. She just moved around with ease and the certain knowledge that things were okay. Being out there with them day after day, I began to feel like that too. Eventually I became certain about life again, and I gained the understanding that no matter how bad things got, life would take care of itself. That feeling has never gone away to this day.

May we be walking beaches together
for the rest of our lives

Take a walk on the beach, just you and the ocean. Take a vacation in paradise away from worry. The beach makes us think, dream, and decompress. Anxiety has no place on the beach. Bask in the ocean breeze and feel an instant mental boost. The earth's natural spa, the ocean, is a healing environment, from the salt and minerals in the water to the fresh air and soothing view. Just breathing in the air near the ocean may help you feel happier and more vibrant. The ocean always seems to be therapeutic, calming your nerves, and also lifting your spirits.

Leading researchers continue to investigate the psychically and physically curative quality of the ocean environment. Some research suggests that negatively charged air molecules are plentiful in the atmosphere near the beaches and will boost your mood, increase your energy, and relieve your stress. Tune in and chill out; listening to the sound of waves is enough to lower your heart rate. No wonder we love the ocean so much.

Finding inner peace at the beach
"He who lives in harmony with himself lives in harmony with the Universe."
—Marcus Aurelius

The most beautiful place on earth is the beach. The beach can bring much-needed inner peace. Just the sounds of the waves and the smell of the ocean help me find my inner peace. My worries wash away with the sea breeze and the sounds of the waves. Simply being on the beach puts everything into perspective. I like searching for seashells as I walk the beach. Every beach adds to my collection and memories. The beach's gifts are endless, but the most treasured gift will always be inner peace. The beach offers us so many opportunities to express our emotions in a more constructive way. You can find yourself and find the answers you are seeking simply by walking along the beach, watching the waves, and listening to the sounds all around you.

The ocean always seems to know how a person is feeling by expressing those emotions. That's why I like to people-watch when I'm at the beach. Seeing people happy makes me happy; seeing people with smiles on their faces make me smile.

The ocean does have a calming effect on people; also, the calm and peaceful beach affects your desire for inner peace. The inner peace deep within your soul knows that there will be more gifts for you the next time you come.

Part 2

Ocean wisdom

Special moments in your life
"Nature is painting for us, day after day, pictures of infinite beauty if only we have eyes to see them."
—John Ruskin

If we take pictures of the amazing beauty of the ocean, sunrise, sunsets, or whatever good times we are having at the beach, we can enlarge the photographs. Then we realize we walk on beauty every day, restoring our sense of hope as we marvel at God's creation. You can live your fantasy and leave your real life behind.

Could you see the colors of your sunrise or sunset? Sometimes we don't have time to see the sunrise or sunset. More of the time we don't even try to see them. Do they still exist?

Do we have no value unless we are working ourselves to death? What belief have we accepted that suggests that, if we are not rushing and hurrying, we have no meaning? We used to live before we become so important. Now we don't have time, and we don't have much freedom of choice, do we? When we are in full joy, we shine like the sun. When we are on vacation, we just count the days.

I cherish every day, every moment, every sunrise, and every sunrise I can see, especially at the ocean. Where else could we possibly want to be?

Seashore of the mind

"Sit in reverie and watch the changing color of the waves that break the idle seashore of the mind."
—Henry Wadsworth Longfellow

Every moment spent at the seashore is a time to break the idle seashore of the mind. When was the last time you spent a quiet moment doing nothing, just sitting and looking at the ocean or watching the waves rippling at the shore? Have you ever spent quiet time observing a sunset by the ocean shore? The ocean has some potent power to make us think pleasant thoughts. Just like the tide of the ocean, the tide of the soul is beyond our control.

Music for the heart
"Music and rhythm find their way into
the secret places of the soul"
—Plato

What is earth's hum? Nobody knows how it is made or what its meaning is. Isn't that wonderful? I enjoy the mystery of God's earth humming to itself, like the roar of the ocean, the vibration of the ocean wind on your face, the different notes of the songbirds, the sound of a heavy rain, or the silence of the spring morning in the park. Earth's humming sounds are great for your mind. They are God singing to creation. Maybe God has left a fingerprint of earth's hum on your soul, too.

The deep roar of the ocean and the notes of the songbird are music to my ears and soul.

God's love notes
"What we are is God's gift to us. What we become is our gift to God"
—Eleanor Powell

God leaves love notes for us everywhere. All we have to do is simply look for them, and we will always find them. They might show up in a beautiful sunset, the sound of an ocean wave, or the sounds of birds singing their song. There is a beauty in everything if we are willing to read God's love notes, which are scattered everywhere. If only we could unplug our ears and open our eyes to the universe, it would reveal itself; it is ours for the taking. We can read God's love letters and then leave them for the next person who comes along to see. Pretty soon those love notes become love letters, and then they become a book for the journey of a lifetime. The universe is ours for the taking.

Wake
What are the wild waves saying?

Get out of the "wake." The wake is only the trail left behind by a boat; it's not what propels the boat. If you apply this idea to your life, you'll see that what you've left behind is not the cause of what you're experiencing or failing to experience today.

Don't rock just anybody's boat

What a world we live in. There is such a communication breakdown that we are starving for trust. We are grasping for handles of lifeboats and waiting for patience. We act out of desperation and discipline, but also quiet patience, as we try not to rock anybody's boat. In hard times, like with today's economy, we are always hoping that things will get better, always wondering what we could do to change things. It has become safer not to know what our lives really mean. Should we focus on the pleasure of little things or even the bigger picture? We have so much fear of facing ourselves and confronting the choices we need to make that we are willing to wreck our lives and the lives of those around us in order not to have to make a choice. We always resent it when others make decisions for us, and we do not want to be responsible for our own choices. Our lives are not set in stone. We have options, and we have choices all along the way. We can choose to rock our own boat. Life is in the living. The process of life keeps happening. Rock your own boat into a life of happiness.

Rushing to calmer seas
"The man who has experienced shipwrecks shudders even at a calm sea."
—Unknown Author

Have you ever noticed that people who live in warm climates are a lot calmer, have a lot more patience, and live more slowly? Imagine starting each day in the fresh air, with no shadows of yesterday or clouds of tomorrow. It is not possible to completely let go of the past and have no concern for the future, but we can stop, relax, and be here. Learn how to live in the present, how to simply be totally present in the moment. How often do we miss our life by focusing on the past, yearning for the future, or never having enough time?

No matter what we are involved with, there is never enough time. We are always frustrated at the time we don't have, and somehow the past and the future were always getting in the way. The past has its consequences; the future has its mystery. We all want the present to be all there is. Have you ever watched people in rush-hour traffic? They are weaving in and out of traffic, holding on to their steering wheels for dear life. What's the big rush? Or maybe the more important question is what you are running from? Life is too short to be spent in the fast lane. Why rush?

The present is all we have. To leave it is to kill it. We miss out on some great ideas when we are rushing around, not to mention getting in traffic accidents. Yet when we stop and notice, the connection with a power greater than us is always there. It has never left us. We have left us. Live as if you are living a life on the beach.

> "Yesterday's history, tomorrow's a mystery, and today's a gift."
> —Alice Morse Earle

Loneliness

Loneliness is often the missing of ourselves. When we are lonely, we need to spend some time with ourselves. Maybe the loneliness and the emptiness we feel in our solar plexus (stomach) is a reminder that something or someone has gone missing, or maybe we ourselves have! Maybe loneliness is one of the ways our inner self communicates with us, letting us know that we need to take time to get back in touch with ourselves. Try as we might, we can never fill up this void with anything outside ourselves, any person, activity, or thing. We can wear ourselves out trying to fill up this hole, but this approach alleviates the feeling for only a short while. Eventually we have to get back to ourselves. We are, after all, why we're here. When we are lonely, it's usually a signal that we need to spend some time with ourselves. The next time you get this signal, try some time alone. The beach is one of the best ways for getting in touch with ourselves. Try it and you will see.

On land or at sea
"For whatever we lose like you or me it's
always ourselves we find at sea."
E. E. Cummings

On land or at sea, entangled in community or independent in isolation, we all share this essential aloneness. And in the journey between the depths and heights that nourish our souls and the touch of others that keeps us sane, we are humbled by the miracle of love. If we are kept out of our native feeling too long, we will not like ourselves. We forget that not everyone can go where we go. No one else can go into our depth completely. We must, each of us, return to our innermost element in order to survive. Or maybe we all have to stop and be at the sea or be on land.

"Your life is not a problem to be solved
but a gift to be opened."
—Wayne Muller

Keep your life simple
"Life is really simple, but we insist on making it complicated"
—Confucius

If you look at the ocean, how simple everything looks. The first step in simplification of life is cutting out some of the distractions. This is great for taking a vacation on the beach. One can see how simple everything looks; there are fewer distractions. In beach living, one learns the art of shedding. You learn how little you can get along with, not how much. Physical shedding begins, which then mysteriously spreads into other fields. One needs less clothing in the sun. Needing fewer clothes to wear means bringing fewer suitcases. Beach living brings peace of mind and so much simplification. After a few days at the beach, one finds serenity. The secret to keeping your life simple is not in getting more but in wanting less. Remember, the idea is to not deny yourself the things you want but instead to free yourself from the things you don't want.

"When you stop needing more of everything, more of what you desire seems to arrive in your life."
—Wayne Dyer

Sunrise

"Few sunrises are greeted as eagerly as those viewed through the eye of love"
—Unknown Author

Sometimes we feel that if everything isn't perfect, we cannot be grateful for anything. We easily fall into an all-or-nothing mentality. When we do, we miss the sunrise and the other forms of goodness that surround us. God has painted a majestic sunrise for us to watch. Are we watching? Do we take the time to relax and watch these sunrises?

If you do, you will be touched with the edge of splendor. Sunrises happen every single day. Are you watching?

"Don't pray when it rains if you don't pray when the sun shines."
—Satchel Paige

Every day is a new sunrise

What's exciting about life is that every morning offers a brand new day, with unlimited possibilities. Yesterday's mistakes and regrets belong to yesterday. Today is a clean slate, a chance to start over, to do or become anything you want, to go for it!

So jump into life with both feet! Go forward, head held high, expecting the best. You may be surprised at how often that's exactly what you'll get.

Rainbows
"Life is like a rainbow. You need both the sun and the rain to make its color appear"
—Unknown Author

If you don't ask for what you want, you'll be chasing rainbows all your life. Rainbows are little miracles. A little miracle is a burst of unexpected happiness. It comes out of the blue to delight us with its complete spontaneity. Today, watch for a little miracle. You just never know where it might be.

The only way to see rainbows is to look through the rain. Don't miss all the beautiful colors of the rainbow while looking for that pot of gold. A rainbow is one of the most beautiful sights in nature. The rainbow is a symbol of renewed hope, and sometimes it's lucky to look upon a rainbow. To see a rainbow, you must stand with your back to the sun; otherwise, it will not be visible. Seeing rainbows bring you happiness and good fortune. Also, they are a sign from the cosmic universe that you are about to have something great fall into your lap!

Rainbows in your environment create good feng shui, which brings positive energy. Each of the seven chakras has a specific function and color (the rainbow colors) that promote energy for a healthy life. The rainbow itself is a symbol of hope and good fortune, a blessed bridge between heaven and earth. As one site (www.lunamiska.com) puts it, a rainbow is "a bridge between the real and imaginary."

A double rainbow is a sign of double good luck. When a double rainbow appears, it means that whatever is coming to you has great meaning to you and that one good thing will happen to you. Each rainbow is unique in its own spectacular way!

Every person sees their own personal rainbow, according to how their eyes interpret light. A rainbow is visible light broken into what we see, the seven colors: red, orange, yellow, green, blue, indigo, and violet. They always appear in the same order with red on top and violet on the bottom, in a main rainbow. In a secondary (double) rainbow, they appear in the opposite order. A rainbow also has relaxing, healing qualities and has a balancing affect to attune your body and spirit.

You can never reach the end of a rainbow, where a pot of gold supposedly awaits. But the symbol of hope and good fortune is still with you. While you're on your way to your pot of gold, don't forget to pick up the silver along the way. Look for the happiness under your nose. Unity helps us to understand that we live in a world where everything is connected to everything else. It's like what happens when all the colors of the rainbow come together as one. We get the most beautiful and powerful white light. How often do we ignore the silver right in our path because we're so focused on the pot of gold? Have you ever watched a rainbow over the ocean? It is the most wonderful sight to see. A double rainbow over the ocean is even better.

"Somewhere over the rainbow, skies are blue. And the dreams that you dare to dream really do come true."
—**Lyrics by E.Y. Harbura**

Watching the ocean

The ocean rejuvenates, renews and heals us all. Do any human beings ever realize life while they live it? While watching the ocean, you begin to relax into the movement and to feel like something that belongs to the tide. Perhaps you wonder aloud at how fortunate you are to have such a beautiful day to watch the ocean.

Some people love traveling to new beaches or places, but I don't think it matters whether we go to new beaches. We are probably all looking for the same kind of things, but from different views of the ocean.

Some people are looking for themselves when they go to the beach, and many people do find themselves. A journey anywhere was really a journey through you. All the answers are within you. Let the ocean be your metaphor for finding your journey, the purpose of your life. Your destiny depends upon your own mental conduct. Never forget that the circumstances of your life tomorrow are molded by your mental conduct today. Do what you're drawn to do today. Happiness is in our own backyards—or at the ocean. You are everything; everything you want to know is within you.

"Life is what happens when you're planning something else."
—Unknown Author

**One must find one's self before one can lose it
"Symbols are the imaginative signposts of life."
—Margot Asquith**

The power of symbols is great. Hold a shell from the beach and see if you can feel the ocean where it came from. Shells fill our memories with the timeless rhythm of the ocean.

Symbols are living mirrors of the deepest understanding but use no words. They call into being all that lives in us and about us. Symbols help us bear witness to the mystery of that which makes us happy. Like a broken shell from a long-forgotten sea, they help us hear the days when we could go back to the beach. As Marc Allen says, "When the worlds you create in your mind connect with your heart, you create what you love."

**"Symbols can be so beautiful sometimes."
—Kurt Vonnegut**

Do not disturb

"Do not disturb; I'm disturbed enough already," Some people appear to have hung such a notice on their brains. Hello, is anybody there? Have you an open mind? Is the window of your soul open for fresh air and sunshine, to smell the salt of the ocean air?

Take the "Do not disturb" sign off your brain and open up to new ideas with an open mind. Supply the necessary mental condition and the demand, the opportunity, or the occasion will present itself to you. Let the ocean be your golden opportunity for new ideas, fresh new starts, and a lot of changes in your thinking. When you are ready, you will find that everything else is ready too. Changing your thinking can change your life.

Setting the right course
"I made the right decisions,
I set everything on the right course, and the reforms are going in the right direction."
—Leah Walesa

You choose the direction and set the sails of your life to work with whatever winds blow. You are free to choose your course in life. You never arrive at a particular direction by accident. Life is a series of decisions that carry us in certain direction. The biggest question to ask when setting your course is, where do you want to go? Where do you want to end up in the next year or years from now? When you don't think about these things, you react to life's winds without purpose or direction. Certainly, there are times to simply drive off in whatever direction suits your fancy. This might set off a wonderful adventure full of wonderful experiences.

While it may not be possible to change your past, you can change your future. While setting the right course, your wisdom is always crying out to bring positive changes to your life. If you want to actually choose where you might end up, then you have to set your course. You're the only one who can steer the ship today, because staying on course has everything to do with the wind if it feels right and the waves if it feels wrong. As long as you go with your gut feelings, follow your heart, and use your head, you'll stay on course. The ocean waves will stir you in the right course, if you are watching the movement of its waves.

Happy sailing to you!

**Is the glass half empty or half full?
"A Pessimist sees only the dark side of the clouds and mopes; a Philosopher sees both sides and shrugs; an Optimist doesn't see the clouds at all, he's walking on them."**
—Leonard Louis Levinson

A half glass of water is never just half full, nor is it ever just half empty. It depends on your point of view. We have good days and sometimes not so good days. If you notice that the glass is half full instead of half empty, you will be happier no matter what is going on. No matter how much is in the glass, it is for that time, in that moment, as full as it's going to get. Right now, let yourself enjoy however full it might be.

The empty part of our glass of life is even more important. The beauty of life is that it is uncertain. Uncertainty reminds us of new possibilities beyond our knowledge and experience. This is an amazingly wonderful part of life.

As far as time is concerned, it's an illusion. Time does not exist. Only the moment is always with us. We should realize the power of the moment, as it can do or be anything we want.

Being in contact with our resources means seeing the glass not as half empty but as half full. Life at the ocean is sometimes sunny, and sometimes it rains. But we can all make the best out of a rainy day.

Checking in with yourself every day
"Take the time to come home to yourself every day."
—Robin Casaryean

What good does it do to sail across the ocean when you can't stay plugged into yourself? Practicing moments of mindfulness can really influence the flow and content of your day. In fact, the more moments of mindfulness you enjoy, the happier, more satisfied, more present, and more clear-headed you will become. Just like taking a vacation on the beach, you will have more time to check in with yourself. It takes time and courage to keep checking in with yourself to see what condition you are in today.

Do a few rounds of belly breathing to pause and check in with yourself and with your thoughts. It is unrealistic to think your dreams, perspectives, insights, and values today are the same as they were last year or even as they were yesterday. Pause and ask yourself, "Am I ready?" This question brings all your energies into the here and now without the mind worrying about the past or future. Take a few seconds of your time to regroup with yourself and go for a walk on the beach. This is a great way to redirect more energy to the internal world rather than the external world and deliberately invite more balance into your day.

"Self is the only prison that can ever bind the Soul."
—Henry Van Dyke

Life is like the ocean flowing

Life is like an ocean flowing. If you don't swim against the current, it will take you away.

Our life and experience may well be likened to the ocean. The ocean is expressed in its flow just as our lives are a continuous flow of experiences. Like the ocean, our life has many twists and turns. The ocean of life brings daily blessings as it is passing by, but there is much going on beneath the surface. Too often we resist the underlying problems and miss the opportunity at hand to learn and to grow. The lessons of the ocean can keep us focused on our journey, whether it's toward inner awareness, change, or peace within us. There are many parallels between the ocean and our lives. If we stand on the shore of the ocean and watch it flow by, we become aware that the ocean never changes but its content is always new. We might say that the purposeful, dynamic quality of life within us never changes, but the content of our experience of living never remains the same. Some days we move aimlessly through life with no map or compass in hand and just go with the flow of life. There is simple wisdom in our life and the ocean if only we will listen. Life will go on because the ocean of wisdom in life never ends.

> **"How can you follow the course of your life if you do not let it flow?"**
> **—Lao-Tzu**

How do we raise our sails to inner silence?

The sun shines freely on all of us. The winds are always blowing. We just have to raise our sails. When we do, those tender winds propel us quickly to inner silence. In the ship of life you can't make port unless all sails are set. How do we raise our sails to inner silence? Through sinking into the inner silence and coming into the present moment, so that our hearts are at peace, we can hear the still, quiet voice of the inner person who is steering us home across at the vast ocean of this world.

Take a few releasing breaths and enter a place of inner stillness. Sink into the silence, asking for nothing and hoping for nothing. Just patiently listen and let go. Or go for a mindful walk on the beach, seeing everything as beauty all around you. This beauty and silence is not a luxury: it is a necessity. Silence is one of the most valuable gifts that we can give to ourselves.

Strong winds never last very long; sooner or later, the winds die down, just like us when we practice being silent. You are the captain of your soul; you cannot make port unless all sails have been set. You cannot expect to reach port if the wind doesn't die down ether.

While in silence you can choose your direction and then set the sails of your life to work with whatever wind blows. Give yourself opportunities for going into the silence every day. You'll never regret it.

The purpose of life
"Everyone has a purpose in life, a unique gift or special talent to give to others. And when we blend this unique talent with service to others, we experience the ecstasy and emulation of our spirit, which is the ultimate good of all goals."
—Deepak Chopra

Finding and clarifying your life purpose and intention can help you move with greater focus and clarity every day. The way to see the purpose of life is to realize that life is forever seeking to express itself. Life's purpose for you is to experience and express what life is like as you. So what is life as you? What do you want to express and experience that is uniquely yours? A great way to start exploring your life purpose and intentions is to stop for a moment and ask yourself, what's important to me, and what are my values and beliefs? Write about these ideas today. Your life purpose is generally a single statement related to the overall reason that you feel you are here. What is the greater purpose behind your being alive? Why are you here in this world? Both life purpose and life intentions can be rich and valuable in helping to move through the difficult times life brings us. In difficult situations, see if your life purpose or one of your intentions can give you direction to navigate through the stormy water. The stormy ocean is like the mind, and the waves are the thoughts. Learn to control the waves of your mind, and the ocean of your mind will become calm.

Ride out the stormy water and find your purpose in life.

There's no time like the present
"We discover strength as a person from the ocean; the constant waves and the changing moods of the ocean can help us learn to live in the present moment."
—Unknown Author

John Lennon said, "Life is what's happening while we're busy making other plans." When I am at the ocean, I measure my peace of mind to determine how much I am able to live in the present moment. If my mind is at peace, then I am in the present moment. What happened yesterday or years ago and what may or may not happen tomorrow or this morning does not matter. The present is where I always want to be, especially at the ocean. When we're busy making other plans too soon, too fast, and not thinking things out, our bodies suffer and our dreams slip away. This is how we miss out on life.

Just like the quote says, "We discover strength as a person from the ocean. The constant waves and the changing mood of the ocean can help us learn to live in the present moment. We allow past problems and future concerns to dominate our present moments so much so that we end up frustrated. We spend much of our lives worrying about a lot of different things all at once. When we are at the ocean, we can take away some of the distractions and be in the present moment, thinking about one thing at a time. Many people live as if life passes them by too quickly, as if they are going to miss the boat. Always rushing into the next thing, no one has a guarantee that they will be here tomorrow.

Focusing on the past or future disorients the body, as it only likes to live in the now. Now is the only time we have and the only time that we have control over. At the ocean, we are surrounded by the sound of the waves, the smell of the ocean air, and the surrounding blue water. Here we can notice how calming it is to be in the body in the present moment. In this state, nothing can influence you. In the present moment, you sail on the water of the calm mind.

"The real happiness of life is to enjoy the present, without any anxious dependence upon the future."
—Lucius Annaeus Seneca

Happiness

"Knowledge of what is possible is the beginning of happiness."
—George Santayana

Allow yourself to gently reflect on the good things in your life. Set your sails with greater confidence, for the new shores you wish to explore will bring you happiness. Happiness, like most of the other important processes of life, cannot be planned. So you can make the days you have be the best they can be. It takes a special gift to understand a way to find happiness. First, go out and search for something that you love, something good for you. Find it and enjoy it. You are in control of the vehicles to happiness.

Sometimes it seems that happiness in life becomes very dependent on external people or circumstances. This results in a life that is ripe for frequent disappointment. Action is the key to breaking this pattern of expectation and disappointment. You have everything you need to live life successfully. What are you waiting for? You get the picture. Think about it and do something about it now. Set off to sail through the rest of your life and believe in yourself. Let the ocean be your guide to focus on the present. Someday your ship will come in. Happiness will come in waves. What are you waiting for? Sometimes the key to happiness is just within reach of the beach.

> **"Happiness is when what you think, what you say, and what you do are in harmony."**
> **—Mahatma Gandhi**

All we need is love
"There is only one happiness in life:
to love and be loved."
—George Sand

Knowing someone deeply is such a treasure from the heart. It opens our hearts to the sky of all time. It lets the song come out of the sea and is like hearing the moon through the ocean. It's like moving the ocean between the shores of your soul.

To love or to be loved is the question. I would have to say that to experience love in ourselves and others is the true meaning of life. Love guides you to your happiest, most fulfilled life. Love is never wasted, and it requires no outcome or results. Love is the essence of our being. When we give love, we always receive more back in return. Love also heals, brings peace, and maintains harmony on all levels. It seems like love is truly contagious. Just look what happens when we extend ourselves in love. Love also has to be balanced with some wisdom. That's why love plays an important part in the life we want to live. To express love makes us really feel wonderful. If we show love to a loved one, we are the ocean. As the ocean flows, love must flow, or else stagnation occurs. We must, then, keep the oceans of love flowing. Allow the love to flow from your heart, and let it flow with abundance. As the Beatles sing, "All we need is love."

"The best thing to hold onto in life is each other."
Audrey Hepburn

The ripples of life
"You can make a difference in the world like a ripple effect just by changing one thought."
—Sheena Stagent

Have you ever thrown a stone into a calm lake and watched the ripples come to shore? God leads us to still water that restores our spirit. In life, your actions are the stones you throw. Thus, to see ourselves clearly, we must see the stillness as transparent as a calm lake. When it is still enough and clear enough, we can see through to the bottom. Have you ever stopped to think that there is nothing you can do to stop the ripples from rolling across the calm surface once they have started? When people are moved to reach for us, they send ripples everywhere. You cannot take back the stone once it's been dropped. All this affirms the need to stay with our feelings long enough for the ripples to settle. You have to wait until the energy of the waves dissipates on its own. No one can escape this. If you didn't want the response, you should not have thrown the stone in the first place. Your actions and words cause ripples of effect in your world. Your water will stir, and your emotions will ripple. The only way we can know if our emotion will ripple is to wait till we are clear as a lake again.

Make sure of the energy you release before you make waves, because you cannot stop them once they've been set in motion.

Only when what is stirred up settles can we see ourselves and one another clearly. Sooner or later we will realize our mistakes. The best time to stop the ripple is before you cast the first stone. There's no taking back, so be careful of the impact you are about to make.

If you're lucky enough to be at the beach, you're lucky enough

Our lives and feelings have a natural ebb and flow. We exist in a continuum of tranquil and turbulent seas. One of our main assignments as self-aware beings is to explore both our high and low tides. It is easy to accept the rhythm of life when we're riding the crest of its waves, exhilarated by its effortless flow. Far more difficult is accepting our low tides, the ebbs and storms life presents. In order to grow in understanding and awareness, we must accept the challenge of exploring our inner tide pools, which are exposed as the ocean recedes. After we are hit with an emotional tsunami, it's very valuable to inspect the tide pools laid bare by adversity. When we can attend to the flow of our lives, rather than let our precious bodies be run each day by raw, unfiltered emotions, things have a tendency to balancing out. Here we can gather the information we need to create an emotionally self-supportive life.

Exposing our vulnerable, wounded areas can prove to be the easy part. Working through them may be arduous and slow but is ultimately liberating. As we grow through the aftermath of loss, we often need the comforting arms of supportive friends and perhaps the guidance of an excellent therapist. Gently explore your tide pools. What vulnerabilities are uncovered in your low times? What strengths? Ask yourself what you can do to support yourself emotionally during life's ebbs and then commit to accepting yourself during both high and low tides. There is a rich sea of knowledge and understanding to be explored when we encourage ourselves to inspect the wonders of our own inner tide pools. These discoveries can become the lifeboats in which we ride out the varying tides of our successful lives.

To be true to yourself

"Voyage upon life's sea, to yourself be true, and whatever your lot may be, paddle your own canoe."
—Sarah Bolton

Many of us are afraid to take the risks that seeing our dreams to fruition would require. Do you have a dream? Will you succeed or fail? Do we leap deeper and deeper into the often-choppy waters of fear? Can we swim with the sharks without becoming one? Do we have what it takes to capitalize on our knowledge, market our wares, and stay afloat in a sea of black, or in the beauty of clear waters?

Often as we are being transformed, we cannot tell what is happening. Let your intuition be a way of helping you to get rid of your fears and learn from them. We all have inner wisdom that we often disregard. Believe in your inner wisdom to help you. We all need to honor our gut feelings by exploring them. Remember to trust your gut, follow your heart, and use your head. God has a purpose here for us all; we just need to find it and believe in ourselves. The magic doors are there to be opened, but often you don't see them even as you are passing through. Set your sails, and let your mind go to the deepest sea and see the clear waters ahead.

"The true vocation of man is finding his way to himself."
—Herman Hesse

The joy of growth
"Growth is an erratic forward movement: two steps forward, one step back. Remember that and be very gentle with yourself."
—Julia Cameron

Nature demands change in order that we may advance. When change does come, we should welcome it with a smile on the lips and a song in the heart. Nature has a great lesson for us about growth.

In order to grow, a lobster must be willing to extrude itself from its old shell. The old shell is hard and inelastic and does not allow for the lobster's growth. After shedding, the lobster is left extremely vulnerable until its new shell hardens. The precarious position in which the lobster finds itself does not prevent it from shedding its shell because, instinctively, the lobster knows that no growth can occur otherwise. We are like the lobster in that most of the time we must become uncomfortable in order to grow. When you are safely in your comfort zone, there is no reason to push yourself to delve deeper and experience more of yourself. When you get really comfortable, the universe is on high alert, looking for opportunities to nudge or, in some cases, push you into a greater experience.

When you emerge on the other side of a painful growth experience, you know yourself better because you have gone deeper into your true nature. While no one enjoys being uncomfortable, you do have a choice about how you will handle that discomfort of growth when it arises.

Journey

"So throw out the buoy lines, sail away from the safe harbor, catch the trade winds in your sails, explore, dream, discover."

—**Mark Twain**

Whether you are drifting through life on a boat or walking on the sands of the shore, each day is a journey, and the journey itself is home. Try sitting quietly and imagining yourself bobbing safely on the ocean of experience we never stop crossing. Breathe deeply and imagine each day is a wave. Enter your own rhythms and evaluate what kind of wave today is. If today is cresting, look about you and take in all that you can see of life.

Preparing for your journey, leave your baggage behind. It's time to set off and sail. Pick a special day. Pamper yourself with a special little gift. If your ship has sailed, be grateful for what was.

Life is a journey.
Happiness is what makes you happy.
Destiny is your life's dream.

The journey of a thousand miles begins with a single step

We are all on an endless journey, but there is only one journey: going inside yourself. The word "journey" derives from the French word for day, "journée." It refers to the time traveled between sunrise and sunset. If we set the intention to discover the divine presence through the journey of daily life, we can awaken with renewed excitement and the anticipation of seeking the sacred in all that surrounds us from morning until night. We see with renewed eyes. As we walk out to a park or the ocean, we will discover where we feel ourselves to be in the presence of the divine. There's an ocean of life inside us. Every day is a journey, and the journey itself is home. Today is a very exciting time in our lives. We are on a wonderful adventure and will never go through this particular experience again.

The greatest journey we will ever take is the journey into ourselves. When we think we know everything there is to know about ourselves, we show our ignorance. When we think we know it all, we miss the point. We can learn, and we need to learn, from all that is around us. It's time to set off and sail with your thoughts. Imagine that you are swimming in the mind of your soul.

> **"It is good to have an end to journey toward, but it is the journey that matters in the end."**
> —Ursula K. LeGuin

Jigsaw puzzle of life

"There are no extra pieces in the Universe. Everyone is here because he or she has a place to fill, and every piece must fit itself into the big jigsaw puzzle."

—Deepak Chopra

Life lessons are pieces of jigsaw puzzles; one of the challenges of our life is to integrate the pieces of our lives as we live them. Life is a process, and we are a process. Everything that has happened in our lives has happened for a reason and is an integral part of our becoming who we are. The pieces of this puzzle are given to you in random order sometimes, and sometimes they are not given in any order. Some things will start to make sense when the puzzles come together, and some more pieces of the puzzle will come your way later in life. Sooner or later, you will end up with a corner piece that suddenly makes it easy to fit several other pieces into the picture. Sometime you can get the whole picture, and sometimes you just get pieces of the puzzle.

Life is truly like a puzzle. Each part of your life, each experience, each person you meet, and each accident that happens to you is a piece of the puzzle. Every day you must try to recognize the puzzle and learn to become fully and clearly aware of each day. All the pieces are there for a reason and will eventually come together and make sense. Everything we go through, whether good or bad, will serve as a purpose for us down the road. A great puzzle can't be rushed. Jigsaw puzzles are made to be taken apart.

Chances are that you have some life lessons you have not fully mastered and some pieces of your puzzle that have not come together, but this is normal. Life is a process; no one understands everything about life. If you continue on the path, you will find that every day new pieces of your puzzle of life bring more clarity and more understanding. Keep your head high and stay focused, and you will solve the puzzle of your life.

Similarly, the ocean has many pieces that are part of one big puzzle, all dependent on one another. The salt water, the fish, the coral reefs, the ebb and tide, the moon, and the weather are all parts of the big puzzle. The pieces fall into place eventually.

> **"Most of the places I've been, I've been a main piece of the puzzle."**
> **—Eric Davis**

**People who come into your life for a
reason, a season, or a lifetime
"Some people come into our lives and quickly
go. Some stay for a while and leave footprints on
our heart, and we are never, ever the same."**
—Unknown author

Sometimes people come into your life and you know right away that they were meant to be there. They serve some sort of purpose, teach you a lesson, or help you figure out who you are and who you want to become.

I am convinced that God brings people together for a reason. Fate governs our destiny. Do you believe that people come into your life for a reason, a season, or a lifetime? The people you meet affect your life.

Here is a true story: I met my friend Loretta in Minnesota. She came to me because she was in a car accident, and I do medical massage in my business as a massage therapist. After talking to each other, we found out that we both lived in Philly at about the same time and went to the same places in Philly and New Jersey. We also lived near each other in Philly. One day she told me that she was going to go back to Philly to bury her mother in Forrest Hills Cemetery. Can you believe that is the same cemetery where my mother was buried too? So I went with her family and friends to Philly to bury her mother and to see my mother's grave. My mother's grave was in the same row as hers, five graves away. It is a 1,500-acre cemetery, and our mothers are buried in the same row. I am now more convinced that God brings friends together for a reason.

Loretta has been my friend for four years now, but it feels like I have known her for a lifetime. Loretta is like a sister to me; we help each other out, and we have so much in common. I spend a lot of time at her Cocoa Beach place on vacation. Her condo there is right on the ocean, my favorite place. See? It's another reason why we were supposed to meet. She is a great friend.

"Many people will walk in and out of your life, but only true friends will leave footprints in your heart."
—Eleanor Roosevelt

Sing your song
"A bird does not sing because it has an answer. It sings because it has a song."
—Maya Angelou

Are you doing what you're meant to be doing? Are you singing your song? Our bodies respond favorably when we're engaged in activities that are fulfilling to us. Each of us has a purpose here on earth. The more you insist on being the person you were meant to be, the more joy you will be blessed with, the way a bird is blessed with a song. When you discover your gift, your life changes for the better. We each have a piece of the puzzle to contribute to life. When we all put the pieces together, the whole world takes shape. Your gift is a big part of why you are here. Always know that your gift is necessary right now; otherwise, you wouldn't be here to give it. What gifts are you here to give to the world?

Your source relays messages that can guide your internal compass and point you in the direction of your dreams. Saint Augustine said, "People travel to wonder at the height of mountains, at the huge waves of the sea, at the long courses of rivers, at the vast compass of the ocean, at the circular motion of the stars, and they pass by themselves without wondering." The more you are able to tune in to your source, your inner wisdom, and your soul, the more you are able to act on this inner knowledge and the more joyful your life will be. This life is about the discovery and the delivery of that greatness. Your life is part of the larger world plan. At the ocean you can set your internal compass and tune in to your inner wisdom, your soul. Then you will have more joy in your life.

Wind clears our heads of clouds
A cloudy day is no match for a sunny disposition

The things that wait in our nature for us to bring them alive are the things that heal ourselves and each other. This principle is easy to see in other forms of nature: stars hold the dark by being light. Oceans keep the earth alive by being wet. Wind clears our head of clouds. The sky may be about you, but it is also inside of you. With every breath you take, you intermingle your essence with the sky and exhale your interpretation of the universe. The sounds of the wind are always on our side, especially at the ocean.

"Sounds of the wind or sounds of the
sea make me happy just to be"
—June Poli

Clear as water
"Ocean: a body of water occupying two thirds of a world made for man—who has no gills."
—Ambrose Bierce

Like clouds moving in water, problems make me forget I am clear. Water reflects everything it encounters. This is so commonplace that we think water is blue when, in fact, it has no color. Water, as ocean or lake or even as the smallest puddle of rain, takes on the image of the entire world without ever losing its essential clearness. Of course, that is not so easy for us, as emotional beings; we are constantly losing ourselves in the image of everything we experience. Nonetheless, the nature of water can help us understand our very human struggles. My life and the tension other people put on my emotions kept me from keeping my head above the water. The ocean with the salt in the air taught me to keep my emotions, to reflect on myself without losing who I am. Though we can never be as clear as water, it helps to remember that we can handle our emotions and face the real problems when the problem comes. Beneath the clouds, water desires only to flow, and beneath our tension and problems, the human being wants only to embrace and soften.

Try to keep your head above water
"We are all in the same boat in a stormy sea, and we owe each other a terrible loyalty."
—G. K. Chesterton

In troubled times, we need to swim in the fast-moving river as best we can, trying to keep our heads above the water. Bad things happen that are beyond our control, but the truth is that life is full of both wonderful and terrible things. Nothing is ever all bad. No matter how bad a situation is, there always is the possibility of good coming of it. Worry never robs tomorrow of its sorrow; it only saps today of its strength. When we let ourselves realize that we are in control, then we can keep our heads above the water and swim to calmer waters for life. There's something very special about the ocean that brings a little magic to our everyday world and reminds us all how wonderful life can be!

"God moves in a mysterious way, His wonder to perform. He plants his footsteps in the sea, and rides upon the storm."
—William Cowper

Waves

The waves are clapping against the shore, and the stars are beginning to shine. When you catch a wave, ride it.

If we can close out the everyday noises so often surrounding us, we can hear the waves, the to and fro of the tides, and the music of the sea. Just knowing that God controls the ebb and flow of the tides gives us confidence that everything in our life is under his control as well. Life is all about ebb and flow. Some things come to you; some things are taken away. But then more and more things come to you. It never stops. Life goes on. Today the sea roars, but tomorrow it may whisper. I hope we will be listening to the rolling waves kissing the shore. But it is the waves, the constant and ever-flowing waves, which calm us, soothe us, and send a message deep into our souls.

Basking in the warm sun and hearing the calming rhythm of the waves calms us. Just a piece of great oceanic rhythms of the waves is deeply reassuring. The comforting tidal rhythm is like quiet living and quiet words. We must all live with the core of inner stillness to be in the present, the here and the now. With time to yourself, the time measured only by the tides seems of little importance. Through the ebb and flow of the tides, life still does go on, thank God.

Rewards from the sea
"The voice of the sea speaks to the soul."
—Kate Chopin

As the reward of being drawn to the sea is to swim with the waves, the reward for being drawn into the depth of another is to feel each other rather than to see each other. On the way, we see what we dream of feeling, but once there, we feel from the inside what we can no longer readily see. The fish can't see the ocean. Your vision will only become clear when you look into your heart.

With all sails set
Allow yourself to gently reflect on the good things in your life, and set your sails with greater confidence for the new shores you wish to explore.

You are the captain of your soul. Living life is like sailing. You're constantly making adjustment and corrections, but once you take the wheel and set your course, you can go anywhere. Trust your gut, follow your heart, and use your head. Discover your gift, and get ready for the greatest adventure of your life. You cannot make port unless all your sails have been set, and you cannot expect to reach port if you are not the captain of your soul.

Living words
"Together we can face challenges as deep as the ocean and as high as the sky."
—Sonja Gandh

I have oceans of regrets about things I didn't say. But I spend a good deal of time with my foot in my mouth as well. What is the point? Words are powerful and never die. They begin to live when we say them. We've all let words escape our unthinking, often unfeeling lips that we wished we could recall. The trick is to be sufficiently awake to avoid saying them in the first place. Words take on a life of their own when they leave your lips.

Resentment

> "We must free ourselves of the hope that the sea will ever rest. We must learn to sail in high winds."
> **Aristotle Onassis**

You've got to give up the ship that weighs you down. When we hold on to resentment, it weights us down like an anchor. We wonder why we feel so stuck and held back in our lives. We tenderly harbor our old resentment and the people toward whom we hold resentment. We periodically throw the people for whom we hold resentment a piece of fresh fish to keep them alive, but we only nurture our anger more. It is as if our feet are stuck in fresh seaweed and there is no way out. Eventually we can see that it doesn't really matter what someone has done to us; our holding onto it is hurting us more than them. If we want to heal, the only way to grow is to let go.

> "To reach a port we must sail, sometimes with the wind, and sometimes against it. But we must not drift or lie at anchor."
> —Oliver Wendell Holmes

Water

"The waves of the sea help me get back to me."

—Jill Davis

The sound of running water has the ability to calm all demons and return us to a level of serenity as nothing else can. Water has so many voices. There is the peaceful gurgling of a brook as it tumbles over rocks and moves to its home, the sea. I make my own water fountains with the seashells I collect from the beach and give them as gifts. My friends love the sounds of the water coming off the seashell, and the sound is very relaxing. Regardless of its form, water lulls us back to ourselves, inviting us to return to hidden inner rhythms that get lost in rushing through life.

The more we are worn by experience, the more of an inlet we become and the more the waters of life wash out of us. This is why tears come more easily the longer we are here. Perhaps wisdom is nothing more than the invisible waters rising within us to swell around the eye as oceans soften land, evidence of that inevitable tide that takes a lifetime to rise. Some of the tears are water within us. We need to ask others at sea, what would you like to see?

Calming the inner sea

The wind causes waves to arise out of the sea. Restless thoughts are the winds that bring waves and storms into your mind. We can calm our inner seas by deciding if we would rather be just happy or just right. This means that we choose to let go of unimportant things that we have a stubborn tendency to gnaw on, terrier-like. When you hold resentment against someone, you're bound to that person with a cosmic link; you can calm your inner sea by choosing to be happy. Allow yourself to float free of resentment. Inner peace creates outer peace. Love and accept yourself when you are right and when you are not. Sometimes this is hard to do, but it is worth it.

> **"We ourselves feel that what we are doing is just a drop in the ocean. But the ocean would be less because of that drop."**
> **—Mother Teresa**

Discovering the sand dollar

I remember the first time I saw a sand dollar—and there were a lot of them in Clearwater Beach, Florida. It was just after a storm at high tide on the edge of the shore. I found about twelve of them, each one unique and delicate. After I saw them, my first thought was to wonder how they could survive in the ocean with the waves crashing back and forth, especially after a storm. Then I was wondering how I was going to get them home in my suitcase without them being crushed into pieces. To my surprise, all but three made it home.

When I was very young, my mother read a book to me about mermaids. I remembered that the book called the sand dollars "mermaid money." I thought that was so funny.

When I was in fifth grade, my class made Christmas ornaments from sand dollars. I remember painting them and using all different colors of glitter to make them sparkly. Then we tied a piece of red ribbon through one of the holes. When I got home from school, I gave my mother the Christmas ornaments made of sand dollars. She was very happy, and she reminded me of the book she read me.

To me the sand dollar is like hidden treasure. Perhaps even the sand dollars are teaching us to find beauty in every bit of sand.

Wisdom in us
"Never mistake knowledge for wisdom. One helps you make a living; the other helps you make a life."
—Eleanor Roosevelt

We live like whales and dolphins, always swimming near the surface of the water and trying to get out. We are always compelled by a light from above that we can't really make out—or can we? Just as the water brushes against the eyes of those creatures as they make their way in and out of the deep, our days shape how we see things. So much is going on in this world at any given time beneath what we show the world—all our feelings, all our thoughts and expressions.

Wisdom for the fisherman
Give a man a fish and you feed him for a day.

The Buddhists say that to be a good fisherman, you must detach yourself from the dream of fish. This makes whatever is caught or found a treasure. We sometimes confuse dreams with dreaming and plans with planning. Plans are useless, but planning is invaluable. The Buddhists say wisdom is like a hungry fisherman. We cast our nets, but we never really know what we will catch, and we never really know what will feed us until it is brought aboard. Then we find the treasure.

Doing nothing else, looking at the ocean

I had a big dog named Duke, a Great Pyrenees, who was one of my important teachers. He used to sit on my deck by the lake and just look. It was difficult for me to see what he was looking at most of the time, so one day I just went out with him by the lake. I sat beside him and *looked*. I sat with him for hours and experienced just sitting and just looking. One sees so much when one just sits and looks.

Duke has since died, and his great wisdom in having taught me to sit and look. Now I spend time at the ocean and just look. I let my imagination go wild.

"Oceans"
by Spanish poet Juan Ramon Jimenez.

I have a feeling that my boat struck, down there in the depths,
Against a great thing, and nothing
Happens! Nothing ... Silence ... Waves ...
Nothing happen? Or has everything happened,
and are we standing now, quietly, in the new
life? Or has everything happened?

The power and glory of the ocean
"Why do we love the Sea? It is because it has some potent power to make us think things we like to think?"
—Robert Henri

If there is magic, it is in the ocean water. I believe that the universe conspires to give us gifts, to confirm that we are on the right path of learning. Our job is to remain aware and available in the moment and to stay open to connections. Sometimes just a walk on the beach can change your thinking and improve your life. Albert Einstein said, "Look deep into nature, and then you will understand everything better." If we could be like the ocean, we could see like the ocean. The ocean always knows what it is called to do in life without anyone telling it.

"Your life is not a problem to be solved but a gift to be opened."
—Wayne Muller

A great sailor story
by Zgardener

A party of shipwrecked sailors was drifting in an open boat on the Atlantic Ocean. They had no water and were suffering agonies from thirst. Another small boat came within hailing distance, and when the shipwrecked mariners cried out for water, the newcomers said, "Let down your bucket."

This sounded like cruel mockery. But when the advice was repeated several times, one of the sailors dipped the bucket overboard and drew up clean, fresh, sparkling water! For several days they had been sailing through fresh water and did not know it. They were out of sight of land but off the estuary of the Amazon, which carries fresh water many miles out to sea.

"We are imprisoned in the realm of life, like a sailor on this tiny boat, on an infinite ocean."
—Anna Freud

A clean ship is a happy ship

"A clean ship is a happy ship." This is an old navy saying. For safety and health reasons, ships must be kept extremely clean. They need a thorough cleaning from bow to stern to be totally shipshape.

My mother would say all the time with a smile on her face, "A clean ship is a happy ship." She also said, "Busy hands are happy hands." My mother would clean house all night long. My sister, my brother, and I would wake up for school, and the whole house would be spotless from top to bottom. Every night she would make sure there were no dishes in the sink and everything was clean. My mother would say that you should always start your day with a fresh start: no mess from the day before and no old newspapers. To this day I always make sure there are no dishes in the sink and that everything is always clean in the morning. This makes a big difference in my life; I can wake up every morning with a fresh start to a wonderful day. My mother was also a firm believer in finishing what you start.

> **Are you lost at sea, or have you missed out on the direction you have sailed?**
> **"Your inner knowing is your only true compass."**
> **—Joy Page**

You are not lost. You're exploring. Are you looking at the map for directions when you're unclear about your destination? It's hard to get somewhere if you don't know where you are going. We all need a compass and faith as a map. Let your inner voice guide you to take the first step toward your destiny. Which way will you go?

Let life be your guide. It is like stepping stones. One step at a time each day holds a new direction. Each day you will get closer to your destination. When you are one step closer to where you want to be, you have found the direction. You have found your destiny. It nudges you step by step to the life that is meant to be. Life is good, and it's getting better one step at a time.

> **"He who loves practice without theory is like the sailor who boards ship without a rudder and compass and never knows where he may cast."**
> **—Leonardo da Vinci**

Create a quiet place
"When nothing is gone, everything is possible."
—Margaret Drabble

Create a quiet place; this might be by the ocean. Sit quietly and close your eyes. Slowly feel your breath within the waves. Create a sanctuary in your mind where you can go to receive intuitive guidance. Your inner guide is always directing you to what makes you happy, healthy, and full of life. Intuition is what you know without having learned it. It is a source of wisdom to guide you through life. Your intuition communicates with you through stillness and quiet, but you need to listen for the inner voices. When you listen to intuition and follow its wisdom, you will be led to a life that is full, successful, and rich with limitless possibilities. When you trust your gut, follow your heart, and use your head, you will have balance on your side.

Intuition can come as an image or in a dream, as a sunset or as a thousand other triggers that might activate your intuitive current. Every one of us is born with an intuition code. It is the wise part of you that knows your purpose in life, and this information will help you make the choices that enable you to live your purpose in life.

A bit of stillness is just what the cosmic doctor is ordering for you now. The ocean is calling you!

Ideas in your mind
Ideas in your mind are like branches
of your intelligence growing new leaves
in the wind of your mind.

Great ideas come when we least expect it. While walking or sitting on the beach, you may experience an "Aha!" moment and find yourself full of ideas and new advancers. Remember to take action on the knowledge you have. Honor it and trust it. Trust your intuitive nature; you will be rewarded for it. Believe in your inner wisdom. Communicate with your intuitive thoughts. Remember that life is taking you on a wonderful new path. You have great ideas, but if you want to be successful, let your inner wisdom help you and guide you.

It also helps to have an open mind to receive your guidance. Let your inner wisdom challenge you to try new things and move in creative directions. Because of your imagination, your intuition will be able to deliver some brilliant new ideas. Be productive, and money will flow in. You will get new, brilliant ideas every day. When you take a walk on the beach, your intuition will guide you toward miracles and let you know which direction will produce the success you seek.

Miracles happen every day. You can create them in your life. Let your thoughts and ideas remain open for new possibilities. God wants you to succeed. He is always sending you new ideas. Thank God for the ideas he places in your mind and my heart. Remember to trust your gut, follow your heart, and use your head.

Progress happens when you aren't looking.

Making your dreams come true
"Dreams say what they mean, but they don't say it in daytime language."
—Gail Godwin

Daydreams are like a wave of the sea driven with the wind and tossed. Most people indulge in some form of daydreaming. You are always thinking when you are not asleep, and you know that it is in the selection of your thoughts that your destiny lies. Do not let your daydreams take the form of an escape from actuality. Some people daydream about all sorts of unpleasant things. See to it that your daydreams are concerned with such happenings as you would really like to find in your life. Know that anything good is possible. Remember the creative power of thought, and your daydream will come true. It is sad to think that so many people are afraid to live the life of their dreams.

Dreams add balance to our lives. Some dreams are hopes and wishes. Our childhood dreams and fantasies are gold mines of possibility. Denying dreams dulls us, but accepting them can energize and motivate us to expand into areas that our hearts have yearned for throughout our lifetimes. Take the opportunity to reclaim your unique dreams. Listen to your dreams, current and past. Honor your dreams, waking and sleeping. Respect the information they have for you. Give yourself permission to play. We need to let the feelings and the messages of these dreams filter deep into us so that we can integrate our wholeness. You have the right to dream and explore possibilities.

> **"Everything is possible to him who believes."**
> **—Jesus**

Open the prison door
"We may have all come on different ships,
but we're in the same boat now."
—Dr. Martin Luther King Jr.

This is one of my favorite sayings. We are all—every one of us—in the same boat, but we have a tendency to cluster together with people just like ourselves. That makes us feel comfortable and safe, but it can also cause our perspectives to stagnate. Stretch yourself and enjoy the feeling that comes from reaching out.

Open the prison door that is holding you captive on your own ship. There exists a mystic power that is able to transform your life so thoroughly, so radically, and so completely that your own friends would hardly recognize you. In fact, you would not be able to recognize yourself. What is this mystic power? The power is really the power of just being you. It can lift you out of a painful life that is holding you captive on your own ship. You can throw open the prison door and free yourself.

This power can do for you what is probably the most important thing of all in life: It can find your true place in life and put you into it. This power is really the power of just being you. The birthright power is just being you. How easy is that? We are all in the same boat, the same ocean water, but why can't we just be ourselves?

The sea of inner peace
"We can never obtain peace in the outer world
until we make peace with ourselves."
—His Holiness the Dalai Lama

The lessons of the sea, both good and bad, have followed me through my life. The lessons of the sea have been mostly good. I have learned that I can lead a more meaningful life of inner peace. When I am facing challenges, I can learn from the sea of inner peace how to face them with a calmer mind. I have lived near water most of my life, and I have witnessed the ocean's power in all its forms. It can bring the simplest beauty in the gift of a shell or the harshest danger from the pull of a rip tide. The waves, currents, and tides of the sea are much the same as the ups and down of life itself. As sailors have discovered, many skills at sea carry a lot of risk and lessons for living a more peaceful life. Just as the ocean can be a mix of tranquility and disturbance, so life can be a mix of calm and stress.

I found inner peace through the sounds of silence at the ocean. Silence is rejuvenation. It allows you to be yourself, to relax into yourself, and to find inner peace. Being at the ocean is such a beautiful thing; you feel you are intensely alive. Just sitting at the ocean in silence with a quiet mind creates inner peace, which is bigger than the mind and body and permeates into all aspects of their being. We all need to spend time in nature. Sitting by the ocean instantly connects us to our true natures of inner peace. It calms the mind, nurtures the body, and connects us to our souls. This process will build a sea of inner peace within us.

"Peace comes from within. Do not seek it without."
—Buddha

Weathering the storm of life
Waves are what the ocean knows to make
of water; the wind carries its lessons and
teaches salt water how to be a sea.

When there is so much happening and so many things moving all at once, it is as if we are caught in a storm. Life's movement and happenings often roll in like a storm and bring lessons in their wake. Most people are constantly struggling to maintain a life full of calm weather. That is the way of life itself. For many of us, life is chaotic every day. We battle against many challenges, trying to move ahead and make ends meet. Our minds are distracted by the waves of experience. We should take advice from the ocean by simply going with the flow.

If we weather the storm and accept its lessons, we can learn to be at peace with ourselves. Even in all the noise and confusion, there is a place where everyone can go to find peace, tranquility, and quiet. We should not let ourselves be swept away by the winds, or drenched by the rain. We need to go where life brings sunshine and calmer waves. Seek the eye of the storm by finding a safe harbor for everything in your life. Remember: a ship is safe in port, and it's also quite useless there.

Go with the flow

When the wind blows too hard, don't try to resist. Just let go with the flow and see where life takes you. There are many times in life when we feel we need to struggle against things that are beyond our control. "Go with the flow" means relax; let the current of life's river carry you along. If you get caught in an undertow, the best thing to do is let it take you. Do not resist, and then swim back to shore once it has released you. To go with the flow is to stop trying to swim against the tide of life's struggles and change. It is possible to swim upstream, of course, but that is too exhausting. Taking the path of least resistance can bring you inner peace, relaxation, rest, and an unworried state of mind. We go against the tide when we try to fight reality and resist change. Sometimes we push and strain for what we think we need or want. Struggling against the changes life brings is not going to achieve anything but worry and stress. But it is like fighting the tide when you aim in the wrong direction. If we go with the flow, we become strong and flexible.

Water flows, and so must you. Taking on a free-flowing attitude allows us to be like water. Don't try to change what you cannot change. The best way to see the changes and challenges life brings is to develop an ability to flow with the tide. If possible, steer your boat along with strong currents, not against them. Fighting the currents is a sure way to get yourself shipwrecked. When you are swimming to calmer waters, you can stop fighting against your choices. Then you can relax, float, and enjoy the blue sky ahead, letting the gentle current carry you forward. It is easier to go with the flow of life and enjoy the journey. You might not know where your journey in life will take you, but going with the flow offers an opportunity for change and growth. So just hang loose and go with the flow.

Soul searching

Your life is shaped by the ends you live for; you are made in the image of what you desire.

Finding yourself is an enlightening experience. Finding yourself is harmonious because you develop the philosophy or belief system that will carry you through the rest of your life. Soul searching means looking inside yourself and deciding if the person you are or are becoming is the person you really want to be. Think about it as you go about your life. Spend good quality time with yourself. Anytime we spend some time with ourselves, we learn something new. Learn to listen to yourself. Finding yourself is a journey, not a destination. There is a lot of trial and error. You will hit bumps in the road, and sometimes you will fall flat on your face. I wish you smooth sailing to discover who you really are.

Life is calling!

Inner silence at the beach
Peace, like an ocean of infinite life, reflects itself through me and calms every turbulent feeling.

Inner silence can be difficult for those of us who are caught up in the hustle and bustle of daily life and the endless mental chatter within us.

See yourself standing on the beach, watching the waves rushing to the shore, and then take a deep breath and return to the ocean. Feel the wonderful cool breeze and breathe in the smell of the ocean's salt water. Imagine that you can feel the calmness that you experience now.

Life is wherever you are. It revolves around you even as it flows through you. Keep the doorway of your mind open. Feel, think, commune with life, and know that it fills you with light. There is a lot of magic on the beach. People are drawn to it, swim in it, play in it, and are calmed by it.

> **"When the mind is still, we can become an instrument of peace."**
> —Eknath Easwaran

Wonder of the shore
"What lies behind us and what lies before us are small matters compared to what lies within us."
—Ralph Waldo Emerson

When we go down to the shore at low tide, we enter a world that is as old as the earth and water. Like the sea, the shore is fascinating. Standing on the beach, we can sense the rhythms of the earth and the sea. To understand the life of the shore, you need to be there early at low tide to watch the currents, the tides, the surf, and the creatures. Surges of life beat at the shore.

The shore at night is a different world. The darkness possesses the crashing waves on the beach. At night you can stand on the beach watching the moon's bright path across the water and see the bright stars above. There is a lot of magic about the sea.

The calm before the storm
"There are some things you learn best in calm, some in the storm."
—Willa Cather

We can't change the wind, but we can adjust the sails. In the process of living, we must observe the weather and winds. In life, a strong wind never lasts very long; sooner or later, it has to die down. The winds have an ever-changing influence on us. A sailor knows that he can't control the wind. But the more skills he has, the better he can stay on course as the winds change and the more comfortable he is with unexpected storms.

We must weather life changes just like a sailor on a stormy sea. We need to maintain our balance and peace of mind. If nature in its infinite wisdom chooses not to blow strong winds all day, then we should also follow this example and stay on course. Just like the wind, circumstances are often beyond our control. The more skilled we are, the more comfortable and confident we will be when life becomes more challenging, like the sailor who has mastered the stormy sea. We must view life with adventure and excitement, just like the sea, with our sails set and the power of the winds on our side. When life brings challenges, we must remember that even on a windy, cloudy day, the sun still shines.

When we are in full joy, we shine like the sun.

**It's never too late to change your course in life
"If you do not change direction, you may
end up where you are heading."
—Lao Tzu**

You often meet your destiny on the road you've taken to avoid it. It's never too late to change course. Whether you are drifting through life on a boat or watching the ocean waves, you are on a journey, and the journey itself is home. Anyone who has sailed for a long distance knows that small changes early on can lead to bigger differences in the destination. Being just a single degree off course can mean completely missing our destination.

Small changes made early in your journey can end up having a great impact on your life. No matter how your journey is playing out at the moment, chances are there is always room for improvement. It is time to plot a new course. Everyone has the ability to change the direction of his destiny. The only way to change your destiny is to continuously apply course correction every day.

The best time to begin steering is right now. While small changes early in your journey can have a big impact, that doesn't mean that you can't make changes later along the path. Remember, an adventure starts off in familiar waters and quickly moves into unknown and unpredictable seas. You'll have to navigate both with equal skill.

Follow your inner compass
"You must not abandon the ship in a storm because you cannot control the winds ... What you cannot turn to good, you must at least make as little bad as you can."
—Thomas More

Think of your life as a sea voyage and yourself as the captain of the ship. In sailing the open ocean, know the destination; one of the key points of navigation is to always know where you are and where you want to go. As you travel on this journey, it is vital to always keep a compass. Without a compass, a ship would be lost.

Life is constantly changing. We must decide what thoughts to keep and what to toss overboard. You may feel lost in a sea of options, but don't let the difficult problems weigh you down. The opportunities will come to you on different scales. This will help bring more clarity to your sea of options. Follow your inner compass to get going in the right direction again. Your wisdom within will lead you to the right path.

"I'm not afraid of storms, for I'm learning how to sail my ship."
—Louisa May Alcott

"The Winds of Fate"
by Ella Wheeler Wilcox

One ship sails east,
And another west,
By the self-same winds that blow,
Tis the set of the sails and not, the gales,
That tell the way we go.
Like the wind of the sea,
Are waves of time,
As we journey along through life,
Tis the set of the soul that determines the goal,
And not the calm or the strife.

Strong feelings are like thunderstorms
Is there calm before the storm in your life?

Strong feelings are like thunderstorms; they have a beginning, a middle, and an end. Just like the strong winds, sooner or later they die down. You can ride them out. Instead of fighting, ride out the storm and embrace your own powerful feelings. Trusting our intuition often saves us from disasters. Observing the forces of nature, it's apparent that things are constantly changing. Even the greatest natural disasters don't last forever.

People tend to get so involved in their emotions that they hold on to them for a long time. We keep harboring those emotional storms within us because we're afraid to unleash them honestly and naturally, like a thunderstorm that will quickly become calm. These kinds of eruptions occur in nature all the time. When there's stress, the earth releases it, and then all is calm once again.

Your life is waiting
Planting a seed of possibilities
"How much of human life
is lost in waiting."
—Ralph Waldo Emerson

Pause for a moment. Take a few deep breaths; let your imagination take you wherever you would like to go. Pretend you are on the beach, just you. Hear the waves surrounding your soul, see the vibrant colors of the crystal clear turquoise ocean water at your feet, and let your mind wander for a few moments. Are you back yet?

When we are not in a hurry, we can take the time to notice the beauty of what's around us. We can focus on what's right instead of what's wrong. We can learn that every situation is precious and brought to us by our own wisdom. There is beauty in supplementing the power of your mind with the wisdom of your soul. Your soul is part of you that is forever whispering to you. It invites you to remind you that peace is our nature. In order to practice being who we are, we can plant seeds of possibility. Whatever has happened is what is. Acceptance means that you are in control of the situation before you now.

Your life is waiting. Try to pause for a few moments. Take a few deep breaths every day just as a reminder to realign yourself to your soul.

"My life is a web of endless possibilities."
—Katelyn Pauls

Let the waves of the ocean carry us
The ocean is so magnificent, peaceful, and awesome.
The world disappears for me when I'm on a wave.

One of the fascinating things about the ocean is the wave. The more we're willing to let the waves carry us, the more they will be able to. The more we are willing to experience a wave as gentle, the gentler the experience will be for us. Let the ocean waves gently invite you to tune in to the rhythms of the earth itself and experience the earth's healing powers. The waves fall on the most impoverished soul. Go to the ocean and listen to the music of the waves; the world, the universe, is talking to you. Let the waves in the ocean carry us into joy and happiness.

Someday we will master the waves of life

Rhythm of life

Now is the time to start making that list on starting to live. Life is a constant play upon itself. The tide has its ebb and flow. Life is what happens when you stop counting time. If you spend your time freely, you will have more of it. That means more time to connect and more time to wind down.

Our leisure time is when we can take our time to do things with freedom and move at a pace that feels right. That is the time for us to just to be and not necessarily do anything. Just to be is an art. This art is bliss when practiced well. How good it is to do nothing and rest afterwards? Dreaming takes place during those relaxed times where nothing is scheduled and we are not focused on our never-ending to-do list. This is where balance comes to play: it is so important in our lives. Balance allows us to step back, look at where we are, and dream about where we would like to be. There is a rhythm and flow to life that, if we can just lighten up, allows us to be in the flow. We may realize that possibly we ebbed when we could have flowed, and we can simply relax again into the rhythm of life.

Start to make your list on starting to live today.

Energy Surfing
"If you do not change your direction, you are liable to wind up where you are headed."
—Chinese Proverb

In Ann Marie Chiasson's book on energy healing she uses the example of surfing, which is a great way of putting it. We are out on our surfboard in life. The water is the shamanic field energy, and the waves are the experiences and events that come to us in life. A big wave of energy comes, in the form of an event or experience. We have a choice to surf it or not. If the mind says, "This wave should not be here!" we become so distracted that surfing the wave is impossible, and we crash with the wave. If we see the wave of energy coming, we can ride it to the best of our ability until the water becomes calm again. We may still crash, but if we do, we then have a choice: get back on the board and surf or sit in the water wondering what happened. We are always surfing these energy waves, both in our personal lives and in the collective energy of the shamanic and unified energy fields. Life is always following the rules of energy, and if we are not connected to these rules, it appears that nothing is happening the right way. Once we connect our personal energy field to the unified field of awareness, then we begin to float downstream, to flow with the current of our life. When we are going with the flow in life, we are moving our self downstream. The flow of the water determines how fast or slow you will arrive at your destination, unless your emotions affect the intensity of the flow. Some people might not realize how much energy they are using to struggle against something that is happening or is about to happen. Your reaction sometimes does not change the outcome of a situation. But your emotions and attitude affect how you can deal with the what-if. You can embrace the moment flowing downstream or wrestle with it upstream.

Cranio-Sacral expresses as a rhythmic motion just like the ocean

Just as the natural forces of the universe generate the rhythmic motion of the universe generate the rhythmic motion of tides and waves within the oceans, so those natural forces, as they spread through the body. There are many rhythms within the body, such as heartbeat and respiration, and then there's the rhythm of the cranio-sacral system.

Within the cranio-sacral there are three principal rhythms, first is the cranio-sacral rhythm that is also known as the cranial rhythmic impulse or CRI, which is the reminiscent of waves rising on to a beach and ebbing away again. Second is the middle tide that has a slower deeper quality, more like waves rolling through the ocean. Third is the long tide that has a profound, distant, spacious, timeless quality, like the tides rising and falling deep within the ocean. As a therapist tunes into these different rhythmic motion is not simply a matter of following movement or feeling a rhythm. It is engaging with a state of being.

In cranio-sacral we tend to talk in terms of waves, tides, currents, fluctuations, and letting your hands sink into the warm fluidity of the cranio-sacral system. Analogies with fluids are often drawn to these terms. First are wavelets and ripples, when you first are tune in, the initial impression you encounter are often experienced as minor movements, like the wavelets, ripples and other minor turbulences that you might find on the surface of the sea. Second are currents, you may encounter pulls drawing this way and that, like currents under the sea. Third are waves, as these patterns release you may feel the increasing emergence of rhythmic wave-like motion, like waves rising onto a beach and ebbing away. This is the cranio-sacral rhythm. Forth are deeper currents that you may encounter more persistent and resistant pulls drawing consistently in certain directions, like deeper, stronger current under the ocean. Fifth are oceanic waves within the context of these deeper patterns, you may feel the increasing emergence of a slower rhythmic motion, like oceanic waves rolling across the ocean. These are the middle tide, reflecting deeper levels of health and being. Sixth are tides that in due course as you settle into deeper and deeper engagement, you may feel a long slow movement like the rise and fall of the ocean tide. This is the long tide. The ocean tides are of course a reflection of the gravitational pull of the moon influencing the whole planet, just as our own long tide is a reflection of the natural forces of the universe. Seven is stillness, as you settle into the deepest levels of engagement, you may reach dynamic stillness, like the stillness at the very depths of the ocean where everything is quiet and still. The value of these fluid analogies is that we can see fluids in everyday life and see how they ebb and flow and swirl, so they provide a useful, visible, recognizable analogy for describing something that is not so readily recognizable.

In cranio-sacral you can follow the system wherever it may lead you, as if you hands are being pulled or drawn toward a particular point, like a continuous current under the ocean. Sometimes you have to allow yourself to be drawn by the pulls within the system like floating with the tide. As the system release into a neutral state, with the wavelets and ripples subsiding and a rhythmic motion indicates that the system is ready to proceed into deeper treatment. Sometimes your attention might seem to be flowing smoothly in certain areas, but then the quality might change and you encounter choppy waters, a stormy sea, or a sense of a boat rocking from side to side, or maybe some turbulence, most of the time the client feeling this in the same way you do. During treatment, if the sea is stormy and there are many waves on the surface, then the priority is to settle the surface. Otherwise it may not be advisable to swim or go out to sea, let alone to dive deep. It may be difficult even to see what lies under the surface. Once the sea is calmer, after addressing the waves and settling the turmoil, and opening up the system, then you can not only see more clearly under the surface, but you can look into a clear calm sea, and also swim more safely, dive underneath, go to greater depths, and explore what lies therein. Every cranio-sacral treatment is likely to involve some sort of evolving process like this it might vary from person to person depending on the weather and the climatic conditions within and around their system, whether it is stormy, inundated by waves, or calm, peaceful, and the rate of progress will also vary depending on the degree of strong currents under the surface. The cranio-sacral system never lies, everybody has a story inside.

(Source from Thomas Attlee book Cranio-Sacral Integration)

Take the ride of your life with the flow and balance
We are all on a journey through life, so we might as well sit back and enjoy the ride

Balance is an ongoing journey; it's like being on a canoe on the ocean. You need to balance yourself and learn to move with the flow. The rhythm of ebb and flow is required to balance. Being in a canoe on is far more tipsy in the ocean. You can't fool the balance and flow of nature.

When you are held down by the waves of the ocean and your need for air, you use all your strength to get yourself to the surface. This also occurs in life, when you are being held down and you can't find your strength. We all need to be in the present and find our strength in life. You miss your life when you are not present. A way to live in the flow is to take charge of your body, mind, and emotions. Just like the ocean, life is always flowing, moving and balancing with the flow of the ebb and tide. So take the ride of your life. Relax into the flow and stay present in the moment. You will never regret it.

Floating on the ocean in a raft
Life is a raft floating on the ocean of awareness

While on a raft floating on the ocean, you can feel life carrying you through many of life's ups and downs. Have you ever gone on a raft on the ocean? Try to imagine what it would be like to float against the current. Step onto your raft and you will begin to flow with the current. It is the flow of the water that determines how quickly or how slowly you will arrive at your destination. While you are seated on a raft, sometimes your mind can play tricks on you. One minute your thoughts were on the beach watching the waves, and the next minute your mind was on work or some other task. I think sometimes you get stuck in time. Your body is somewhere, and your mind is in the present moment. In life, our emotions affect the intensity of the flow. As you move with the current, your awareness sometimes brings up some unresolved emotions from past experiences that still have life in you.

Life has its ups and downs. Sometimes the highs can beat the lows. You need to open with the flow again and find a safe harbor. If you are feeling unhappy with your life, you're most likely been going upstream, and you need to get ready to change your direction. Sometimes your awareness contains a lot of negative thoughts that you didn't create but that somehow have landed in your thoughts. Going with the flow of the water helps connect you with the element of water, releasing any emotional blockages that may have settled into your body and leaving you with a greater sense of energized relaxation and calm. Life will always be waiting for you to reenter its currents of awareness. Isn't life amazing?

Life on the beach is your playground
Life is your playground of happiness

Life is a playground. Life will always be waiting for you to seek out some kind of adventure. Sometimes life can be so draining that you feel you don't have the energy to keep going. But if you can jump start your life's adventures. Think of how abundant your life could be. At the ocean there can be rain and a lot of storms from time to time, but after the storm everything becomes calm again, and the energy of the ocean is abundant and lively once more. Similarly, after our energy is drained, we can pick ourselves up and come back full of life and energy again. What are you waiting for? Take an adventurous vacation, explore a new beach, see something new, and find a new playground. Life is good; enjoy it every day.

Part 3

Life at the beach

Vacations

"Nobody needs a vacation so much as the man who just had one."
—Elbert Hubbard

On vacation, I was sitting at the edge of the water to find my rhythm. When I was planning my annual vacation, it was the ocean that called me—not so much to be in it as to be by it. Relaxing and soothing, the comings and goings of the tide set my reset button. You know, the one that connects you with the universe and that gives you permission to get away? Whenever you go, you're only a few hours or even moments away from being connected to the entire universe.

What a beautiful thing a vacation is. Whether we travel to some faraway, exotic ocean or spend time alone at home, vacation allows us time to pause and renew ourselves. Sometimes while on vacation, or after returning, we get an opportunity to take inventory of our lives, to reassess. While we can do this in daily life, somehow vacations, with their extended time for play, rest, and relaxation, provide some degree of distance from daily life to give us more perspective. We get to remember what's important to us and to dream a little. Vacations, in addition to being fun, also create the space for self-examination and reflection. They provide an opportunity to pause and correct course if necessary. To live in balance seems to require both activity and rest in parallel measure. At the beach each moment is dynamic and spontaneous. As you remain in the flow of life, at the beach you will find a way to get sunshine and fun into your life. The sun's rays will dissolve your inner barriers to feeling fantastic and living the life you really want to live. Vacations also let your mind wander.

Most of us spend our working hours on focused mental activities, thinking about specific problems and solutions. Our minds never get a vacation except when they are asleep. But our minds need time off too. We need to be able to "space out" every day, to get wide and wondering rather than just concentrated and alert. That mental space is where new ideas are generated, where we find creative solutions to the problems plaguing us, and where we reconnect to what's most deeply important to our souls. While our minds go on vacation, we can indulge in the pleasure of meandering. Just let your mind go wherever it wants, with no goal in mind at all. I usually get my best ideas that way. Take a few minutes and then come home to your body, and you'll find a surge of enthusiasm and ideas. Intellectual improvement will arise from leisure, and your creative energy will be increased.

You will learn some important lessons when you're relaxing on vacation, as in the quote that I love so much by Richard Carlson: "When you have what you want [inner peace], you are less distracted by your wants, needs, desires, and concerns.

It's thus easier to concentrate, focus, achieve your goals, and to give back to others."

Retreat! Listen to the voice of your soul. When you are relaxed, there will be no wanting in your life. You will know great happiness. Vacations are an extended period of time during which you relax enough to break out of your ruts and routines. When you explore the freedom to joyously create whatever life you want, taking a vacation gives you practice in the very skills you need. Vacation is an opportunity to completely get out of your routine. Vacations offer you a different view of life by taking you someplace else and letting you do things that are completely different from what you normally do. This breaks up places where you may be stuck in your thinking and doing.

When you come back from vacation, you are better equipped to see and engage your everyday life in the same way you engaged during your vacation. This medicine is not only good for you but tastes and feels great! Enjoy your vacation time.

Spring break
"Spring is when life's alive in everything."
—Christina Rossetti

With all due respect to teachers, your kids will learn as much during a week at the ocean as they would in school, and they'll remember it longer. Schedule a vacation with the kids.

Life is a beach, when we're having fun.

Sunrise

"Few sunrises are greeted as eagerly as those viewed through the eye of love."

—Unknown Author

We spread our minds like trees to accept knowledge arriving like the sun, not to instruct us but to warm us and help us grow. Sometimes we feel that if everything isn't perfect, we cannot be grateful for anything. We easily fall into an all-or-nothing mindset. When we do, we miss the sunrise and the other forms of goodness that surround us. God has painted a majestic sunrise for us to watch. Are we watching? Do you take the time to relax and watch these sunrises? If you do, you will be touched with the edge of splendor. It is one of those perfect moments you know you'll never be able to recreate. Sunrises happen every single day. Are you watching?

"Sunrise"
by Ninon de Lencios

Today a new sun rises for me,
Everything lives,
Everything is animated,
Everything seems to speak to me of my passion,
Everything invites me to cherish it.

Every day is a new sunrise

What's exciting about life is that every morning offers a brand new day, with unlimited possibilities. Yesterday's mistakes and regrets belong to yesterday. Today is a clean slate, a chance to start over, to do or become anything you want.

So go for it! Jump into life with both feet. Go forward, head held high, expecting the best. You may be surprised at how often that's exactly what you'll get.

Swimming the ocean

"Most of us, swimming against the tides of trouble the world knows nothing about, need only a bit of praise or encouragement, and we will make the goal."

—Jerome Fleishman

Some people swim in the ocean or a lake to clear their minds. Also, some people say that they come up with the best ideas while swimming. You are more buoyant in salt water compared with fresh water. The ocean is a wonderful playground. It should be respected but not feared. However, the ocean is wild, and potential dangers exist there, such as getting knocked over by a large wave, getting stung by a jellyfish, cutting your foot on a shell, or getting bitten by a shark. The majority of ocean creatures are harmless to people, but some animals occasionally do injure people. Usually, when an ocean animal hurts a human, it is behaving defensively like the jellyfish that stings. Remember that when you swim the ocean you are a guest in the ocean and its creatures. Every wave signifies a new challenge, and everyone has to learn to ride the waves. With a heart that embraces sheer luck and joy, you can swim through life and emerge a winner when you swim the ocean.

Walking and jogging on the beach

> "My life is like a stroll on the beach …
> as near to the edge as I can go."
> —Henry David Thoreau

I like to take short walks down the beach with bare feet. I like the feel of the sand between my toes and the feel of the ocean water also. I think walking the beach is very relaxing, and it is also great for people-watching. While walking, you can capture the beautiful view of the ocean along the way. You can also stop and pick up some beautiful shells, but if you are going barefoot watch out for jellyfish and broken shells.

If you get too hot, you can always jump into the ocean to cool yourself, especially while jogging. I find that jogging on the beach is easier earlier in the morning because there are not a lot of people around. Walking and jogging also give you more energy, and it is nice to get some fresh ocean air.

Don't forget to take a bottle of water, a hat, and sunglasses. And make sure you put on some sunscreen.

> "Run hard, be strong, and think big."
> —Percy Cerutly

Watching Sunsets

> "Sunsets are so beautiful that almost seem as if we were looking through the gates of Heaven."
> —John Lubbock

Take time to watch the sunset. Sunset has always been one of my favorite times of day. Before I simplified my life, I was frequently too busy to enjoy it. Now that my world is simpler, I almost never miss what is regularly one of the most spectacular show on earth. There's something so captivating about the setting sun, especially when weather and atmospheric conditions help to create dramatic cloud formations and brilliant colors that give your whole world a different hue. Seen in the light of the setting sun, our problems seem more minor, even if only for a few moments. The wonderful thing about sunset, like sunrise, is that it happens every day, and even if the sunset itself is not spectacular, it marks the beginning of the end of another day. It's a great time to pause and take notice. Teach your kids to enjoy the beauty of sunrises and sunsets, too. It a very inexpensive show, and it's a whole lot better for them than television. Over the ocean you can see the best sunrises and sunsets. Watching them is a great way to start and end your day.

> "May your time be filled with relaxing sunsets, cool drinks, and sand between your toes."
> —Unknown Author

Solitude
One must go alone and every day

We all need quiet time every day, and it is up to you to make it happen. We need a daily dose of solitude to gather ourselves. If you have yet to savor this treasure, put it high on top of your priority list. Quiet time is like food, water, and air; we all need it to survive. Solitude is good for you, and it gives you a more positive outlook on life. Moving into the silence requires that we shred all expectations while knowing that our answers are there. A place of silence is a place beyond thinking and reasoning, with open anticipations. You can do a meditation practice in which you dedicate an hour, or just twenty minutes, to quieting your mind and body. Find a place in every day to take your body on vacation.

I usually spend twenty minutes in the hot tub or sauna or just take a few minutes to breathe fresh air in the morning or take a walk in the park with my two dogs. If I am on vacation at the beach, I enjoy the sound of the waves and the breeze of the ocean. I enjoy take a walk by the seaside to recharge my batteries and renew my contact with nature.

This form of solitude not only invigorates us physically but also renews our spirits, soothing any bruised emotions and stirring up new creative energy. This quiet place offers information and wisdom, and it is available to all of us. Silence heals and nourishes us all. Can you steal some alone time every day?

Time for me
Go to the beach where you can embrace your solitude and silence

Every day when I am on vacation, I like to just sit on the beach and enjoy my own company. It seems like there is never enough time for myself. Sometimes I even have to schedule an appointment with myself to just be alone. Time is free, but it's priceless. I would rather be enjoying it. Sometimes you can't count every hour in the day; you need to make every hour in the day count. Sometimes I have to hit the pause button so I have more time for myself.

The quieter you become, the more you see, feel, and hear yourself. It's easy to get caught up of images you see outside yourself. Your higher self is always calling to you to wake up to who you truly are. When you are in doubt, be still and wait in silence. Silence is necessary for the soul's nourishment. There is a difference between being in silence and being quiet. Silence is the place in which your soul can grow and expand. Spend time in the silence and you will discover your own company and simply enjoy being with yourself. It is easy in solitude to live after our own selves. When you schedule time for yourself, you do things that are important to you. For me it is being at the beach with myself.

Be with yourself by yourself

Ocean ritual

There's an ancient Celtic ceremony involving a circle of stones. Basically, you form a circle of stones and sit inside it until your answer comes. In Celtic mythology, stones hold a rich concentration of power; they are believed to contain mystical properties. A circle of stones acts like a pressure cooker, focusing and containing energy. This could provide the boost you need.

First, you will need to collect a number of large stones from the shore. On the morning of the full moon, signifying the peak of a cycle, collect some purple sage (which in Native American tradition is associated with purification).

Sit cross-legged on a blanket in the center of the circle and burn the sage in a round ceramic container. Close your eyes and ask for guidance. Meditate and watch the ebb and flow of the waves. You can contact a truer voice inside and follow your heart.

The beauty of this ritual is the freedom it offers—freedom to explore what you really want from life. It allows you to define new directions and to clarify your visions and desires, even if you may not know what they are. It's a way to become centered, to stop giving away your power, and to take responsibility for it. Implicit in all ritual is self-respect as well as honor for a spiritual reality, however you define it. This ritual requires the faith that guidance is available. Such faith is essential for everyone who is preparing to see. Ritual helps instill this by illustrating time and again the depth of change that is possible when we act on what we know within us.

Conch shells

The queen conch's shell continues to thicken throughout its life, and its blood appears blue because it contains hemcyanin. Queen conchs are prized for both their edible meat and attractive shell, and they are useful as fish bait. They live in the sand, in sea grass beds, in coral reefs, and in warm, shallow water. The Florida fighting conch is named for the mollusk's aggressive nature and ability to sting as a defense against other marine creatures. Conch shells can be used a wind instrument, just like a trumpet. The Hawaiians use the conch to play a ceremonial fanfare.

Life on the ocean wave
"Life is a wave, in which no two consecutive moments of its existence are composed of the same particles."
—John Tyndall

Waves are like pieces of music to the ears of a surfer. There are many types of surfing waves, which makes the sport very challenging. Every time you go on the open water, the waves may bring you a great surprise. Never go surfing if the wind is blowing from the direction of the shore. Weather could be a surfer's best friend or worst enemy.

I rented a surfboard on one of my trips. I was told only two rules: no more than one person per wave, and never turn your back on the ocean. The ocean reveals itself gradually. When you are out just fifty feet offshore, it's clear that being in the ocean and looking at land provides a very different view. When you are in the ocean and there are rain showers, the raindrops striking still water sound like bells. The ocean has a message sometimes. If you count every seven wave and it is a great wave to surf on. Also when you are surfing, you can feel more in tune with yourself, and it is like reaching a state of personal balance. Let your mind become the surfboard and move effortlessly through the ocean of your mind.

Tranquility

"The more tranquil a man becomes,
the greater is his success, his influence,
his power for good. Calmness of mind is one
of the beautiful jewels of wisdom."
—James Allen

Tranquility is relaxing into the calm ambiance of a beach, with emerald-green waters and sugar-white sand. A tranquil mind is paradise found. It is harder to find the more frantically you search for it; relax and let it find you. Stillness and tranquility set things in order at the ocean. Believe in yourself, and then you can delight in tranquility. It is the garden in which your soul can grow. There is enough tranquility for everyone to enjoy, but each must make his own journey to find it.

How can we find tranquility in today's world? It's difficult with cell phones, computers, and iPods. Having peace of mind and inner calm are well worth the effort. One of the enhancers of tranquility is solitude, time spent in a relatively isolated place like the ocean that is free of outside noise. Life takes on a deeper meaning and becomes more fulfilling when you have tranquility and solitude.

Think of tranquility as utter calm. Visualize a calm ocean, with no waves, no boats, no wind, and nothing but still water as smooth as a glass surface.

> **"When you find peace within yourself**
> **you become the kind of person who**
> **can live at peace with others."**
> **—Peace Pilgrim**

Beach walk

During my morning walks alone toward the ocean, I sit down on a rock or in the sand and gaze ahead to where the clouds and waves come together. The sun is a bright red ball in the sky, and there are a lot of men casting fishing lines. Whether it's gray and angry or olive green before the rain or sapphire, I never get tired of watching the ocean or watching all the seagulls flying about.

When I walk at lunchtime, the noon sun glitters on the ocean, and a collection of silver water shines across the ocean. Whitecaps roll in parallel lines and break into froth upon the shore. The silence is broken only by birdsongs and the rush of the wind.

In my evening walks I see the sun setting over a deep blue strip of the ocean lining the horizon. At night I love to watch the first star and say, "Star light, Star bright, the first star I see tonight. I wish I may, I wish I might have the wish I want tonight" when making a wish.

"A Day by the Ocean"
by Melissa Robertson

As the ocean waves at me and the sand greets the sea.
The fish swim free and shells wash up by me.
The sand squishes suddenly between my toes, then
the tide flows over them and back down it goes.
The salt is on my tongue, the ocean song is sung. The
sun is going down and so my day at the beach is done.

Just relax and listen to the waves

If you are looking for a small time commitment, check out www.donothingfor2minutes.com. You'll find a picture of the ocean at sunset, the sound of waves, and a timer that will count down two minutes. If you touch your mouse or keyboard while the timer is going, the word "fail" will appear on the screen, and the timer will reset. Close your e-mail before you begin. At first it may feel like the longest two minutes of your life, but it is well worth it to look at the ocean and hear the waves. You can also download this on iTunes for free.

For a sunset screensaver, go to www.beachsunsets.com.

An undersea effect to help children sleep

It's a struggle faced by many parents: getting children to sleep at night. The Tranquil Turtle from Cloud B lends a helping flipper by combining three sleep aids in one: a plush toy, a night light, and a music box.

The turtle creates an underwater effect with tiny lights that shine beneath its opaque shell. The lights revolve slowly, casting a shimmery, aquamarine scene across the ceiling. The turtle also plays a tune or, for parents who prefer ambient sounds, the soft rumble of distant ocean waves.

To save battery power, the turtle shuts off after twenty-three minutes. There is no option for continuous play. A timer that could run for at least an hour or two would be a nice addition, because children often wake up the moment their music shuts off.

The Tranquil Turtle is priced at $55, but it can be found at retailers like amazon.com and Bed, Bath, and Beyond for around $40. Or go to www.cloudb.com.

A dolphin story

One morning, while sitting and watching the ocean, I saw a pod of dolphins swim by. I had always wanted to swim with the dolphins and thought this was my chance. As I ran into the ocean, I noticed my body freezing up with fear and my head was questioning the wisdom of this action. My mind was quite convincing, pointing out that these were wild animals far bigger than me who could hold their breath a lot longer. This was water, not land. I had to decide whether I was going to follow my gut feeling or my heart.

I think in the course of our lives, we often come to a point where we must choose to follow our fears or follow our hearts. We are the decision makers. No one else can tell us which direction to take. I chose to follow my heart. When I did, my body relaxed, and I could hear the playful dolphins. The dolphins surrounded me, and I could tell that they were my best friends. They somehow knew that I was not going to harm them; they just nodding as if they were saying good-bye and swam away.

It is a magical experience to watch the dolphins play. When I am having a hard time or when I need some guidance, I call the dolphins to guide me and protect me. They help me to see that I shouldn't take life so seriously all the time. I believe that each of us has a guardian animal that watches out for us and comes to us when we need them. For some it is a dog or a cat; mine are the dolphin and the eagle.

A little bird story

A small bird travelled thousands of miles across the Pacific unencumbered and alone, needing only one piece of baggage: a twig. He could carry the twig in his beak, and when he got tired he simply descended to the sea and floated on it until he was ready to move on again. He fished with the twig, ate with the twig, and slept on the twig. Who needs the Queen Mary? He flapped his wings, clamped his life raft in his mouth, and set out to see more of the world. What a life. I wonder if that bird ever got lonely. But even if he was alone, he seemed to perceive the proper direction for his life.

Birds seem to have innate compasses that guide them wherever they wanted to go. They seem to know just exactly what they are and how to live. But do they have feelings? Do they fall in love? Do they cocoon themselves off with only one other bird as though it were the two of them against everything? Birds seem part of everything: space, time, air. No, how could they shut out the world if they wanted to fly over it? Have you ever felt as if you were suspended over the earth and dipped and flowed with the air currents, just like the bird?

A duck story

A monk was sitting on a bench next to a lake when he saw some ducks swimming in the lake in front of him. The ducks were feeding on things in the water. Suddenly, the silence was broken when two ducks started to fight. These two ducks were quacking away at each other, flapping their wings, jabbing at each other with their bills, and making a lot of noise. Perhaps the noises they were shouting at each other said things like, "Why did you come so near to me? I do not like your smell. You are invading my private space. Go away!"

That's what we humans might have said. After about thirty seconds or so, the two ducks stopped fighting and settled down as suddenly as they had started to fight. One duck swam a short distance away to the left while the other swam to the right. When the ducks were a safe distance away from each other, both suddenly stood up on the water with their webbed feet and started to flap their wings vigorously. They were literally standing on the water, and then they stopped. It was then peaceful and quiet, and all the ducks went about with their feeding as if nothing had happened.

According to the monk, if the ducks had human minds, the fight would have lasted a bit longer. One of the ducks would have continued to carry the grudge, feeling sad, and perhaps told others about it. Instead, the ducks flapped their wings to disperse the negative energy that was built up during the fight. When there was no more negativity left in the ducks' bodies, they could live happily ever after. The lesson we should learn here is to let go, cleanse, and clear negative energy immediately after such an incident. There is really no point in complaining about a quarrel and continuing to carry it in our body. Carrying this negative energy will only be detrimental to our physical and mental health.

A little starfish story
The boy and the starfish
by Unknown Author

A man was walking along a deserted beach at sunset. As he walked, he could see a young boy in the distance. When he drew nearer, he noticed that the boy kept bending down, picking something up and throwing it into the water. Time and again he kept hurling things into the ocean. As the man approached even closer, he was able to see that the boy was picking up starfish that had been washed up on the beach and, one at a time, throwing them back into the water. The man asked the boy what he was doing, and the boy replied, "I am throwing these washed-up starfish back into the ocean, or else they will die through lack of oxygen."

"But," said the man, "you can't possibly save them all. There are thousands on this beach, and this must be happening on hundreds of beaches along the coast. You can't possibly make a difference." The boy looked down, frowning, for a moment and then bent down to pick up another starfish. He smiled as he threw it back into the sea and replied, "I made a difference to that one!"

The man had nothing to say and left. He continued to walk on the beach but was unable to get the picture of the little boy out of his mind. It was a moment of truth and deep soul searching and self-confrontation. In time, he returned to the star thrower and joined him, silently throwing back the starfish. Together they sought to save, sensing intuitively that man cannot exist spiritually without life.

You make a difference today!

Part 4

Ocean facts and creatures

Boat facts

You need to know this:

The **port side** of a boat is the left side of the boat.

The **starboard side** is the right side of the boat.

The **bow** is the front of the boat.

The **stern** is the back of the boat.

Natural navigation

A natural navigation method is to use the sun and other celestial bodies as a guide. The sun, the moon, and all the stars appear to rise east and set in the west.

The sun really stays in one place. It looks like it's going down because when the earth turns around to the moon, it goes under the horizon.

Sometimes, depending on the season and the lunar cycle, the moon will appear lower in the sky, or it may rise at an earlier or later hour. These variations make it possible to see the moon during the day at certain times.

According to scientificamerican.com, looking at the sun can make you sneeze because it dilates the eyes very quickly, which causes a sneeze. Aristotle said that the heat of the sun on the nose was probably responsible. The philosopher Francis Bacon's best guess was that the sun's light makes the eyes water and then that moisture seeps into and irritates the nose.

A little fish story

The instant fish accept that they will never have arms, they grow fins. I was surprised to hear this one day.

Starfish

Did you know that when a starfish loses an arm, it grows another?

Jellyfish

Jellyfish live in all oceans, and you will find many floating along the shoreline. You should avoid going to areas where jellyfish are sighted or where there are dead ones lying on the beach. Their sting is quite painful. The first aid for a jellyfish sting is to liberally douse vinegar on the affected areas. Jellyfish are fascinating creatures, and there are a lot of interesting jellyfish facts. Did you know that jellyfish are considered a delicacy in some countries, including Japan? Another fascinating fact about is that they don't have any brains, hearts, bones, or eyes.

A tiny species of jellyfish may have achieved immortality. Once it reaches sexual maturity, it is able to revert to a sexually immature state through cell transdifferentiation.

Sea snakes

You're likely to see sea snakes if you spend enough time along the Pacific coast of South America. What are they doing there? Dying, most of the time. If sea snakes spend too much time in direct sunlight, they dehydrate and die. The real reason they're at the beach is because they're weak, sick, and dying of old age.

Sandpipers

Sandpipers are often seen running near the water's edge. I always think of them as the cartoon character Roadrunner. They have relatively long legs that they put to good use, just like Roadrunner. They feed on insects and worms. They retrieve them by pecking and probing the ground with their short bills.

A big shark story

Sharks get a bad rap. Some people are terrified of sharks, as of the ocean, but we can look at them in a different way. Sharks, like dolphins, can teach us to stay awake. The main thing to remember about sharks is not to go swimming when the ocean is churned up and murky because sharks have poor eyesight. People are not the food source of sharks. Most shark attacks happen by accident, and the chance of being struck by lightning is far higher than the chance of being attacked by a shark. Sharks can hear a fish in the water from more than a mile away.

Humpback whales
A whale of a good time

"Spiritual" is the only word that adequately describes how one feels in the presence of a whale. Observing whales in Maui, Hawaii has given me an unforgettable thrill. Maui is the best offshore place to whale-watch and was a highlight of one of my vacations. The best time to whale-watch in Maui is January to mid-April. No one can say for certain what the future holds for these special whales, whose journey has taken them so far. But I, like millions of others, am hoping that after all these years they can adapt and thrive in the wild and become truly free, as nature intended from the very beginning.

Seeing a whale, even at a distance, is just so gratifying. They are intelligent creatures that share the planet with us. I hope it will always stay that way.

Seahorses

Seahorses are truly unique, and not just because of their shape. They are among the only animal species on earth in which the male bears the unborn young. Unlike most other fish, they are monogamous and mate for life. They are found in shallow tropical and temperate waters throughout the world. Because of their body shape, seahorses are rather inept swimmers and can easily die of exhaustion when caught in rough seas.

Lobster and shrimp

If you're dying to know if you're about to eat a male or female lobster, all you need to do is look behind the legs and before the swimmerets (an abdominal cavity in females for carrying eggs) for a small pair of appendages on the underside of the lobster. If these appendages are hard and boney, it is a male. If they are soft and feathery, you've got a female. You have to look closely; sometimes they are folded up under the body.

Shrimp live in oceans all over the world: near shores, in cold waters, in tropical waters, and in the deep sea near the ocean bottom. Some kinds of shrimp burrow and make snapping sounds with their claws. Some shoot bubbles that stun prey with sound waves.

Dolphins

Dolphins are great teachers. They are free spirits who display considerable care and intelligence in their interactions; they are models of how we could be in our own lives. They are among the strongest animals. They can use tools to solve problems, very much like apes.

Bottlenose dolphins will surround a mother as she is giving birth to protect her from predators. One among the group, an "auntie" dolphin, might also nudge the tail of the emerging calf and give whistles of encouragement to the mother.

Eagles

The bald eagle is a sea or fish eagle and has been the national emblem of the United States since 1782. It has also been a spiritual symbol for native people for far longer than that. Always look for them soaring in solitude and gracing the sky with ease.

It takes about a hundred days for eagle hatchings to become independent of their parents. It takes one mating pair of eagles ten years to breed just two breeding birds.

Horseshoe crabs

As they grow, maturing horseshoe crabs shed their shells. The shells are made of chitin, a material that does not stretch. While the new cuticle thickens and strengthens, the crab is very vulnerable, so it molts in protective deep water.

Pelicans

The life of a pelican seems to be a very lazy, if not a very pleasant, one. Pelican live in flocks; they also sometimes help one another to feed. Female pelicans lay two to three eggs, but it is rare for more than one chick to survive. Oldest siblings get first dibs on food and often kill smaller chicks by pecking them or throwing them from the nest.

Ocean birds

Seagulls and egrets are just a few of the birds that make their home near the coastline. Who could blame them? I would love to be near the ocean and fly too. You will rarely see a young seagull, for their parents are very protective and continue to feed them for quite a while.

The moon

All the bodies of water in the world reflect the same moon. It belongs to all of us who see it reflected there for a transcendent moment, no matter who we are or where we are. The moon belongs to us all. Watch for the moon reflected in water. Think of everyone in the world. The moon's gravitational influence produces tides and a minute lengthening of the day.

Full moon

The full moon represents hope for the future. The full moon is on the exact opposite side of the Earth from the sun. The full moon is a celestial treasure itself.

Did you know that when there is a full moon, writers are more creative?

Harvest moon

The harvest moon is the first full moon after the first frost.

How lunar cycles affect tides

The tides at a given place in the earth's ocean occur about an hour later each day than the day before. Since the moon follows the same rhythm, it was long suspected that the moon was associated with tides.

Minnesota Snowbirds

Minnesota snowbirds are typically retirees who are sick and tired of the very long, cold winter. Starting in November they flock to Arizona, California, Florida, and Texas. They even have a Minnesota snowbird club. You can join the early bird gatherers in planning the season.

Every winter, they recreate to a more sunny regions of the south. Some carry their homes with them in the form of campers, RVs, and boats.

These are people who scoff at living in warmer places because they would never want to miss out on the change of season. I would not like to live where it is over 100 degrees, either.

Living in Minnesota in the winter is a blessing and a curse. A recent storm bringing fifteen inches of snow reminded us of why we call it "MinneSNOWta." But when we live in Minnesota, snow is part of our DNA. It's a little like growing up in San Diego and complaining about the ocean. Here in Minnesota we need to survive the winter with some sense of humor. The true secret to surviving a Minnesota winter is good shoes, a warm coat, and a few trips to thaw out your soul. Sometimes it is even too cold to snow here in Minnesota. At Christmastime, jingle bells are frozen. Here we have a winter wonderland with lots of things to do: ice fishing, snowshoeing, sledding, cross-country skiing, sleigh rides, snowmobiling, etc. We also have a winter carnival with ice sculptures and outdoor bars made out of ice. There is plenty to do in the summer, too, with our ten thousand lakes—water skiing, tubing, etc.

Those who live in Minnesota will give the shirts off their backs (but not in the winter—just kidding!) That's why we are called Minnesota Nice: because we are.

Here is a hot flash in Minnesota: beach ball–sized hail. Just kidding!

Part 5

Life's good

The ocean is calling you!

Sailing

**"The winds of grace blow all the time.
All we need to do is set our sails."**

—Ramakrishma

The winds of circumstances blow on us all in an unending flow that touches each of our lives. Sailing can inspire you. You catch an invisible force, the wind, and off you go. What guides us to different destinations in life is determined by the way we have chosen to set out sail. Your destination may be straight ahead, but if the winds are not going in that direction, you must tack from one side to the other, moving yourself incrementally closer to your goal.

The way that each of us thinks makes the major difference in where we arrive. Though many sailors leave from the same harbor with the same wind, each will choose his own journey and destination. The major difference is the set of the sail. We each come into this world from the same realm, armed with different possible journeys, destinations, and adventures, all awaiting our choices. We have all experienced the same divine winds. We can navigate on course or off, with the same intentions in mind, and yet arrive at such different places. If we stop paying attention, the winds will push us in whatever direction they are blowing. It may not be where you want to go, so navigate wisely. We all have challenges to face, and disappointment happens to us all.

Happy sailing!

Kayaking

> "The river delights to lift us free, if only we dare to let go. Our true work is this voyage, this adventure."
>
> —Richard Bach

Kayaking makes for an exciting pastime, especially if you like fishing for redfish, sea trout, and a lot of other fish that are good eating. You will have to fish the tides. Storage is one of many very important aspects to kayak fishing. There is obviously a limited of storage space on a kayak, which should include a life jacket, fishing rod, assorted tackle, bait, water, cell phone, and sunscreen.

What most people enjoy about kayak fishing is being surrounded by natural beauty in pristine environments. Your mind, body, and soul filter out everything except what is going on directly in front of and around you. If you kayak in Florida, the dolphins and manatees can appear at any time. Kayak fishing is an awesome way to fish in almost any inshore body of water. If you kayak to a bird sanctuary, you will see thousands of birds scattered along the shoreline. Bird watchers can view southern bald eagles, reddish egrets, white pelicans, great egrets, great blue herons, little blue herons, and a lot more. Kayakers can also encounter alligators, fish, stingrays, crabs, jellyfish and otters. When kayaking near the land, you might see wild hogs, deer, black bear, raccoon, and bobcat.

Kayaking itself is very enjoyable and exciting. The scenery can be very beautiful. If you go in early evening, you can also catch some beautiful sunsets. All of this can create a stress free, worry free, and healthy environment for most people.

Surfing

Surfing is a way of life for a lot of people on any given day—rain or shine, spring, summer, fall, or winter. You'll find devoted and passionate surfers along the shores on every beach from Mexico to California, Florida, and Hawaii. Most surfers are waiting very patiently for the perfect swell and ride.

After great surfing, as with a wonderful workout or any energetic activity in which the body feels good and the soul comes alive, you have a heightened sense of well-being. As everyone who has ever been on a surfboard in whitewater knows, surfing is a very difficult sport. It takes a lot to learn how to read the waves. In this state of clarity, you feel an excitement about life and increased energy to meet adventures. It reflects back to you the possibilities and potentials you would never know unless you unleashed the power of the wave moving through your world.

Learning to surf is a challenging process. Your friends are there to encourage you, to help you up when you wipe out, and to hoot, howl, and celebrate your awesome ride. Waves satisfy all surfers, and the energetic flow of the wave is an indescribable experience and adventure. Wouldn't it be nice to have this feeling every day? I'm sure you have lots of reasons for not taking time daily to energize your being.

Snorkeling

Snorkeling is relaxing and easy to do. Swim the calm waters and observe the thriving life below, and don't forget you underwater cameras.

Snorkeling in Mexico

A spectacular underwater landscape awaits as you snorkel along the miles of world-famoureefs in Cozumel, Mexico. Cozumel hosts over five hundred species of vibrantly colored tropical fish and coral, and there are miles and miles of incredibly clean, pristine reefs with mountains of living coral.

Snorkeling in Florida

See Florida through a snorkel mask and you'll discover awesome shipwrecks. The Florida Keys are a good place to discover snorkeling spots because of their crystal-clear waters.

Snorkeling in Hawaii

Hawaii has the best snorkeling beaches ever, and you can see the most amazing tropical fish and sea life there. You can also swim with the dolphins, bask with turtles, and glide with manta rays. Maui is far the best island for snorkeling because there are many swimmable, beautiful beaches, great weather, and beautiful, clear, calm blue water. In the winter months you can also watch the humpback whales right from the beaches

So happy snorkeling wherever you go!

Coral reefs

Coral reefs are underwater structures make from calcium carbonate secreted by corals. They are colonies of tiny living animals found in marine waters that contain few nutrients. Often called rainforest of the sea, coral reefs are home for 25 percent of all marine species.

Try scuba diving beneath the surface of the ocean. Swim through spectacular sea arches and watch the wonderful underwater ecosystem and the coral reefs.

Enjoy a massage on the beach
Life happens when we are relaxing
the mind and body together

Enjoy a rejuvenating massage on the beach, in the warm tropical breeze. Outdoor massage in a warm climate melts away stress and tension. Relaxing in the open, fresh air and listening to the sound of the waves makes you clear your thoughts. It is like taking your mind on vacation, giving you a sense of peace and quiet. After years of working with massage clients, I know that to heal the body, ideally you want the mind going in the same direction that the body goes. If that's not working, then it's time to turn the mind off. Even if you see the massage as nothing more than giving your mind a one-hour vacation from your body, just letting your worries be put on hold for a one hour will access a place of stillness that will be wonderful for you.

Massage outdoors can be a journey in more ways than one; it can take you on a restorative path of awaiting both mentally and physically. That one hour is when the sounds of the world surrender to the body that can access your mind. In finding this place of stillness, you can reclaim your own rhythm and hit the "reset button," and letting your mind go off to wherever your thoughts would like to go. Hearing the ocean during your massage will stop time just long enough for you to regroup and balance your mind, body, and spirit. Your beach massage will relax your tired, sore, tension-filled muscles, stimulate your circulation, and help you leave your worries behind.

Start getting into relaxing beach massages. Your body and mind will never forget their appeal. Massage reminds your body of the pleasure of taking time out.

"Lose yourself in nature and find peace."
—Ralph Waldo Emerson

Craniosacral therapy in the ocean
Enjoy the gift from the ocean
and the touch of the ocean

Craniosacral therapy was developed by John E. Upledger in 1970. Craniosacral therapy (CST) is a gentle, hands-on approach that releases tension deep in the body to relieve pain dysfunction, help the immune system, and improve whole-body health performance.

What happens in the ocean or water during craniosacral therapy? When the client is floating, the body can move in a loosening manner that promotes changes in tissue mobility and tension. The therapist simply follows and supports this movement with her hands. As the tissues release restrictions, they will come into greater functional alignment and will help lengthen or soften the tissues. With a greater movement of the tissues, the fluids and the structures will allow the client to move in a more functional way. This supports the body's own self-corrective mechanisms. Water is healing and also reduces gravity and friction, making movement almost effortless. As joint range of motion increases, the nervous system is able to move into a more relaxed state. The healing process begins to work more effectively when the muscles lengthen, tensions release, and internal natural healing improves. The rocking motion of the ocean combined with the water's energy allows you to access a more relaxed client.

It's a humbling experience to witness a healing journey. The ocean is always willing to wash away what we are willing to let go so we experience peace, harmony, and wellness. Floating not only induces a relaxed state but also allows us access to our subconscious mind, which helps past traumatic experiences to surface and be released from the mind. When floating underwater, you can become aware of how your body feels and pay attention to your craniosacral system. You can feel how your brain feels with more freedom and also how you spinal cord feels when it is moving freely with less gravity. Salt water is also a reminder to our minds of our first environment before we were born.

Everything we do in the treatment room is multiplied when working in the ocean or water. The ocean adds that extra element that can gently urge clients toward their next stage of healing.

Craniosacral therapy can also be done lying on a flotation bed in the ocean.

Go with the flow and let go of control

Meditation by the beach
Take the journey inward and discover the waiting treasure

A Tibetan Buddhism, Lama, compares the thoughts that rise in meditation to waves that rise from the ocean. It is the ocean's nature to rise.

The ocean waves calm the body and mind. The sounds of continuous ocean waves on a beach are perfect for relaxation and stress reduction.

Ocean mindfulness meditation is a great way to develop a peace of mind and acceptance of the present moment. It helps us develop inner body awareness. Thoughts are like the breath and the ocean waves; they both rise and fail. When the waves settle down, then you can instantly recognize the silence. When the mind is always thinking, it is always active; when it stops thinking, silence happens, and the mind is in pure awareness.

There is much we can learn from the ocean. It can represent our inner silence. The sounds of the ocean are spiritually soothing, and its salt can purify our physical selves.

Most of us don't have the luxury of living by the shore or visiting the beach on vacation. We can resort to a CD with ocean sounds to help us slip more deeply into a mindless meditation. Try sitting quietly and visualizing the ocean. Use that mental image as the starting point. Just as the ocean tides sweeps the shores, you will restore your balance. Your mind will be clear.

Breathing on the beach

Feeling come and go like clouds in a windy sky. Breathing consciously is our anchor.

The intoxicating fresh ocean breeze just makes you want to take a deep breath. Did you know that you could improve your blood pressure, energy levels, heart function, and even mood by simply breathing?

Here are some important facts about breathing. Breathing is energy. When energy flows through the body properly, you are in a state of relaxation. This is the most fundamental truth of the body, the mind, and our health. If your energy is flowing properly through breathing, your meridians are clear, your aura is clean, and the chakras are balanced. Then your body is functioning properly and is in a blissful state.

This will help you get started breathing on the beach:

While sitting on the beach, create a little seat out of the sand, sitting cross-legged on it. Close your eyes and surrender to the eternal peace. Now inhale and exhale deeply through the nose a few times. This helps clear and calm the mind as well as relaxes the body. I like to think of inhaling positive things and exhaling negative things out of my mind. Allow the breath to flow calmly and easily through your body, feeling a blissful connection with your surroundings. Listen to the sound of the waves of the ocean. Feel the gentle breeze on the skin. Melt and dissolve into the natural rhythm of your breathing, and trust that your body is a unique expression of the divine wisdom. Now you are warmed up. Now that you are all balanced and relaxed, it time to go for a walk on the beach. You will have a different outlook on life, and you will be more relaxed through the day.

Yoga by the ocean
"The body is your temple, keep it pure and clean for the soul to reside in."
B.K.S. Lyengar

I love to start my day with yoga on the beach in the early morning just before the sun comes up. The ocean waves roll gently in the cool morning breeze, and that is enough to relax anybody's body. I think that your body loves being connected with the ocean's energy. Just by sensing the power of the ocean, your mind will begin to expand, allowing you to see the bigger picture. When we're doing yoga on the ocean, most of us feel calm and free, which helps us stay centered and balance. That is what I really treasure the most.

You can breathe in the fresh ocean air and also be supercharged with sunshine. Just think of enjoying the fresh air and sounds of the ocean waves while opening and purifying your body. This opens our bodies, minds, and hearts to the rhythm of the ocean waves.

Yoga also increases inner strength, flexibility, and mental awareness. This creates more energy, relieves aches and pains, and improves your lung capacity and endurance. Just focusing on your stretches can help to relieve tension make you feel stronger, more agile, and calmer. After your yoga session, you can rest your eyes on the ocean, which brings a sense of tranquility to your body, mind, and spirit. Yoga on the ocean builds an inner connection with the element of water. This will help in releasing any blockages or emotions that have settled into your body, also leaving you with a sense of ease and calm. The ocean setting is the key to your success. There is simply nowhere better to be. I guarantee that you will have a beautiful start to your day and a peaceful practice by the ocean.

Riptide
Avoid losing your life; patience permits us to cling to our faith

Rip currents are responsible for about 150 deaths every year in the United States. In Florida, they kill more people annually than thunderstorms, hurricanes, and tornadoes combined (source: northeastsurfing.com).

When a wave breaks on a beach, the water that runs up on the beach soon reverses course and flows back down the beach to the ocean. This is called the backwash. Backwash from the bigger waves can be very dangerous at any time. This backwash can drag you down and drag you out. When it flows back to sea, it is a riptide or a rip current. This rip current can move along the top of the water and pull you straight out into the ocean. This rip current can knock you off your feet even in shallow water. If you get knotted around and disoriented, you may end up being pulled along the bottom of the ocean. But if you relax your body, the current should keep you near the surface. Above all, don't give in to panic. It is easy to say "stay calm," but it is hard to do. But the bottom line is that being calm is what will save your life.

Undertow

When the undertow grasps us we will realize that we are somehow being carried forward even as we tumble

While in Hawaii I got caught in an undertow. In the ocean, when a strong undertow gets you and you are being sucked down to the ocean bottom, you just have to let go and go with the flow. Do not panic. You'll exhaust all your strength by attempting to swim against it. The most common wisdom says to relax and let it pull you out past the turbulence. If you swim parallel with the shore, that will allow you to get back to the shore and get into calmer water. It takes a lot of trust to ride out the currents going in the opposite direction. An undertow is basically spinning you around as if you are in a washing machine.

Sometimes in life, you just have to let go and go with the flow. Stop fighting and know that you will soon be on solid ground. Life has a way of pulling you down, but you need to stop, look, and listen to what is happening and go with the flow. Maybe that's what they mean in Hawaii when they say, "just hang loose."

Seasickness

According to H & M Landing, seasickness starts with the inner ear, your balance center. Even though your head aches, you are sick to your stomach, and you basically feel the worst you have ever felt. You are not really sick; you are just out of balance. You will feel very bad at first, but you must remember you just have a motion problem. You can do a lot to cure yourself, and very quickly.

The first thing you might do is turn around in a circle until you fall down and throw up. If you stop turning, you will feel better very quickly. Your balance center was just out of whack.

The second thing to remember is that fresh air is good, but you want to stay low and to the stern of the boat. That is where you will encounter the least motion. The bow of the boat pounds through the waves, up and down; the stern drags through the water. The ride is much smoother there. The boat rocks from side to side. The higher you are, the more movement you encounter. Also, you can move to the boat's center of gravity to eliminate motion due to translation.

The third thing is to look directly at the fixed shore or the horizon and try to get your balance. The fourth thing is to take some deep breaths. Rock your shoulders back and forth. Try and roll with the boat instead of subconsciously stiffening up and fighting the motion.

It's called getting your sea legs. Sometimes a nap will help. Also, try to take your mind off how bad you feel and focus on something else, such as reading a book.

A fifth thing is a natural remedy of sucking on crystallized ginger, sipping ginger tea, or taking a capsule of ginger. Also, there is a ginger drink called Smooth Sailing that many people say works quite well to settle the stomach.

In the future, you can find a seasickness band online before you leave. Severe seasickness can be treated by using a combination of both the scopolamine patch and Bonine, but you should check with your doctor. The side effect is hunger and more drowsiness. To be effective, this medication should be in your system eight hours before you board the boat.

No-see-ums

Now you feel them, but most of the time you no-see-um
Avoid being bugged by their bites

The no-see-um obviously gets its name because it is nearly invisible, small enough to crawl through window screens. Also known as sand fleas, no-see-ums breed like crazy. On the beach, no-see-ums will most often bite your lower legs or your ankles just because they're closer to the ground. But if they pass through in a swarm, then your whole body will be attacked. Be alert when you're sitting at the beach or outdoors. No-see-ums wake up when the sun goes down and are most active at dawn and dusk. The first line of defense is dousing yourself with at least 30 percent DEET, cactus juice, or Avon Skin-So-Soft. I also heard of a combination of lotion with lavender (they hate that) with vinegar and water (spray your sheets and yourself). Using a fan when you are sleeping helps too.

You won't see um, but they will bug you!

When was the last time you really looked at the ocean?

When was the last you really looked at the ocean? When did you last look at the sunrise over the ocean, see the beauty of the clear blue sky over the ocean, or smell the fresh air in the morning? What about looking at the marvelous sunset over the ocean or seeing the moon and the stars gaze over the ocean? These are experiences that we sometimes take for granted. We forget to see the beauty of the everyday. Every one of us lives under the stars, but do any of us look up at the sky anymore? Do we really touch and truly taste life to the fullest every day? Every day you wake up with another day of life. But when was the last time you truly looked up at the stars or really experienced what we are missing out on every day in this marvelous world?

With the death of my father and with the loss of some family members and friends, I started thinking that we don't get another chance in life like this one. Don't wait for one last look at the ocean, the stars, the sky, the moon, the sunrises or sunsets, or even a loved one. Look now, as soon as you can, and think about the beauty of the world every day when you wake up. When was the last time you really, truly looked?

Good-bye to the ocean
"The longer I live, the more beautiful life becomes."
—Frank Lloyd Wright

Thank you.
Linda J. T.

About the author

I am a person who loves the ocean. I have been studying the ocean since I was very little. I was born in San Diego, California, and moved just about every year due to my father's relocation while he was in the US Navy. All my life I have lived by the ocean or have taken vacations by the ocean. Every day by the ocean has brought self-discovery and extraordinary changes to my life. I have done a lot of soul-searching while at the ocean for many years. *Oceans of wisdom* is all about paying attention to the process of life and taking joy in the journey. I currently operate my own massage business in Minnesota, which I have owned for seven years. I am committed to spreading health, wellness, and the pursuit of happiness and relaxation.

CPSIA information can be obtained at www.ICGtesting.com
Printed in the USA
BVOW082258120513

320438BV00002B/3/P